3·15·78

Sydney Foott

Handicapped at home

Handicapped at home is a Design Centre book. The series aims to provide the consumer with practical advice on equipping and planning the home, and there are also titles covering special aspects of design and planning.

Other Design Centre books are:
Planning your kitchen
Planning your lighting
Children about the house
Rooms for living
Planning your bathroom
One room living
Rooms for recreation
Planning a town garden
Setting up home

Forthcoming:
Colour and pattern in the home

Front cover photograph
by Homer Sykes

Back cover photograph
by Timothy Quallingron

Handicapped at home

Sydney Foott

a Design Centre book
published by Quick Fox

Handicapped at home
First edition published 1977
Second impression 1978
A Design Centre book published
in the United Kingdom by
Design Council 28 Haymarket
London SW1Y 4SU

Designed by Anne Fisher
Printed and bound
in the United Kingdom by
The Whitefriars Press Limited
London and Tonbridge

Distributed throughout the continents of
North America, including Canada, and
South America by Quick Fox, 33 West
60th Street, New York, NY 10023

International Standard Book Number 0−8256−3090−8
Library of Congress Catalog Card Number 78−51872
© Sydney Foott 1977

Contents

Acknowledgements

My acknowledgements are due first to Selwyn Goldsmith, both for his personal help and for his book, *Designing for the disabled*. All handicapped people owe him a great debt.

Next to Elizabeth Fanshawe, who helped with advice on the draft. She is the most recent of my handicapped friends, from whom I have learnt so much over the years.

To my friends and colleagues at the Disabled Living Foundation and the Design Council, who have contributed to my education.

To Mrs Annabel Rowe and her two children, also to the tenants of the Havinteg Estate, Tottenham and the John Grooms Association for the Disabled, Finsbury Park, for very kindly allowing us to photograph them at home.

And finally to Jenny Sturtridge, my long-suffering secretary, and to Nicola Hamilton and Anne Fisher, editor and art editor, who made my work so pleasant.

Sydney Foott
May 1977

Introduction

'A machine for living': is that *really* the definition of a home? Originally hailed as a profound truth, Le Corbusier's dictum has been ridiculed in recent years. But for handicapped people a home must be functional, otherwise it is useless. Many able-bodied people accept – possibly with grumbles – conditions in their homes which they find uncomfortable, inconvenient or frustrating, but few of them bother to take positive steps to set matters right. However, if they become disabled, or if a disabled person shares their house, then the home must be planned accordingly; a source of annoyance to an able-bodied person can be a total barrier to a disabled one.

Where a house or flat is designed for someone with a particular disability it can be tailored exactly to his needs according to the funds available. More often, however, a home is shared between a disabled person and an able-bodied one, or with a disabled person as one unit in a family, and with a limited budget to effect alterations. In these situations, as is so often the case with design matters, there must be a compromise. However, while some modifications will be needed for an individual, the main requirement is for a generally well designed house, in accordance with known standards of function, including those of safety.

This book tackles the problems facing a family that includes a disabled person, and provides guidelines for a happy shared life. The general considerations relating to different types of disabled people are discussed first. The main principles covering flooring, lighting, heating and ventilation are dealt with next. The subsequent chapters deal with

common-use areas, where comparatively little adaptation or allowance is made; rooms where equal attention must be paid to the needs of both able-bodied and handicapped people (notably the kitchen and the bathroom, each of which is essential to the independence of the disabled user); and those rooms where there are specialised requirements for the disabled individual and which may well be his own personal domain. (For convenience 'he' is used throughout, although of course both 'he' and 'she' are applicable.)

Safety, which is of equal importance to each type of user, is dealt with separately. The chapter on special equipment and appliances also covers handles and controls, communication and transport. Both visual and aural communications are vital to a disabled person, and may well involve special planning. They include those for convenience, such as a door-answering and opening device, and door controls generally; the telephone; and the pros and cons of an alarm system. Transport is important, but the actual vehicle (car, adapted car or tricycle) is not discussed here as it is not part of the home. Details of the garage (access, size and type of door) are given in Appendix D. Recreation, covering workshop, garden, greenhouse and pond, is an important part of family life, and is dealt with separately.

Finally, independence – the driving force which lies behind the successful effort by a handicapped person to live a normal life. Often the efforts are immense: a disabled person may find jobs take longer, are painful or tiring, more complicated or more difficult than an able-bodied person would. It is therefore necessary to plan the living conditions well, to make the jobs more

possible and enjoyable for the disabled person, in co-operation with his able-bodied companions.

The appendices give details of useful organisations, both those which give general advice and help to handicapped people (such as the Disabled Living Foundation and the Royal Association for Disability and Rehabilitation) and those connected with particular illnesses or disabilities (British Rheumatism and Arthritis Association, British Polio Fellowship and so on); addresses of suppliers of aids and equipment; details of wheelchair requirements; and suggestions for further reading.

The aim throughout is for as much independence for the disabled person as possible, and for a happy life shared with the rest of the family. Obviously the adaptations and adjustments needed will depend on the type of disability, the age of the disabled person and his role in the family. Specialised aids will be needed, for example, for a person without hands or with the use of only one hand. In other cases, either some equipment must be used solely by able-bodied people, or help must be available for certain parts of the task. It may be necessary to have assistance in transferring from chair to bed, bath or WC, or getting into the car. Much can be done with sensible planning, using commercially produced appliances and equipment. Other specialised aids are available, some through the National Health Service, others from a variety of sources. Details of some of these are listed in Appendix C, and information can be obtained from the Disabled Living Foundation (Appendix B).

Chapter 1
General considerations

In adapting a house to include the handicapped member of the family, the type of his disability is probably the most important factor although, as with all the family, age, tastes and social habits are important.

For the disabled person there may be special needs; sometimes this will entail a more rigid interpretation of design principles, and sometimes a particular variation. Steps are one of the most obvious problems; for an able-bodied person they are probably no hardship, but for some disabled people they may put part of the house out of reach. The same distinction applies to heights and widths; shelves or controls placed above or below normal reach may be a source of irritation to an able-bodied person, and involve either the use of a set of steps (more often precarious balancing on a chair or stool) or kneeling down on the floor to reach the back of a cupboard or a skirting board socket. But for most disabled people, whether they are ambulant or in a wheelchair, such a setting makes the storage or appliance completely useless. The problem is the same with the controls on cookers and heating appliances, opening and closing windows, and the type and siting of taps and of handles on doors and cupboards.

The difficulties associated with space are more specific. For some disabled people, particularly those with arthritis or who have suffered strokes, distance is associated with fatigue and possibly pain. For a wheelchair-bound person space may be immaterial, or may in fact be advantageous, in that there may be more room to manoeuvre. Indeed, in some situations adequate space is essential for a disabled person: to transfer from a wheelchair to the WC, for example, or for getting into and out of the bath. People in wheelchairs have special space needs in corridors and doorways, in order to ensure the easy passage of the chair. Appendix D gives the width necessary for wheelchairs normally used in the home, and further information is available in *Designing for the disabled* and *Four architectural movement studies* (see Appendix E).

Children
While the general considerations in the book apply to young disabled people, there are some specific problems regarding children. It is probable that they will be away from home during the day, either at school (day or residential) or at a play group. They need a sense of their own identity, and for this reason their independence should be encouraged in every possible way, both by providing privacy in their bedroom (shared or individual) and by encouraging their integration into family life and duties. The arrangement of the bedroom is discussed in Chapter 6. The kitchen (Chapter 4) should be designed so that every member of the family may do his share of the work, whether it be preparation of meals, washing up, or laying the table. A child does not remain a child forever, and will eventually have to cope with a varying number of household chores. Play space is vital to a handicapped child, and if this can be planned so that it is attractive to an able-bodied child also, so much the better. A disabled person is the object of so much 'receiving' that the more he can give to others the happier he will be. All children need companionship, and non-handicapped children from the neighbourhood should be encouraged to share recreational facilities, particularly if the disabled child is at a special school, so that he and the other children learn to integrate at as early an age as possible.

The photographs of children used throughout
this book are taken from Mark's wheelchair
adventures by Camilla Jessel (Methuen
Children's Books, 1975).

9

10

Old people

The needs of older disabled people (and what age *is* an 'old' person: 65, 70, 80, 90?) are much the same as those of a younger person. Old people may possibly tire more easily, and therefore distances should be short; they may be more liable to incontinence, and therefore every help should be given by providing easily accessible toilet facilities; they probably want to be able to retreat from family noise occasionally, so a self-contained bedsitting room (with its own television set and some simple cooking facilities) is essential.

The blind and partially sighted

A well designed house, with as few changes of level as possible, is usually suitable to blind or partially sighted people. Certain special aids and appliances are helpful (such as, for example, scales with weights rather than a dial), and electric hobs and fires are safer than an open gas flame. Controls on cookers and heating appliances can be brailled (these can usually be appreciated by non-braille readers), and advice on any changes is available from the Royal National Institute for the Blind (see Appendix B). Help and advice is also available from the low vision clinics (see Appendix A).

The deaf and hard of hearing

In general a well designed house suits deaf people, with emphasis on visual, rather than aural, signals. This applies particularly to communications (telephone, door and so on), which are discussed fully in Chapter 8. Specific advice on aids and appliances is available from the Royal National Institute for the Deaf (see Appendix B).

Brailled controls and other adaptations for gas and electric appliances are available from local showrooms. This central heating programmer has been adapted for the blind.

Incontinence

If a disabled person — whether adult or child — is incontinent, several general adaptations must be made. Any flooring in shared or purpose-built rooms must be washable. In shared rooms this can be managed by a protective mat under a chair or wheelchair, but this is obvious and humiliating. An upholstered chair used by an incontinent person must be covered in a waterproof material, and various plastics are suitable. It will probably also be necessary to provide some form of deodorant. Beds require special protection, and advice on this and allied problems is available in *Incontinence* (see Appendix E).

Epilepsy

The main risk here is of fire, and for this reason there should be no unguarded fires in the house. It is probably wiser to cook by electricity rather than by gas. Sharp edges to furniture are also a danger, and possibly too unguarded staircases. Further specific advice is available from the British Epilepsy Association (see Appendix B), and the various problems are discussed in the chapter on safety (page 38).

Chapter 2

Flooring, lighting, heating and ventilation

A well designed home must be efficient and safe to run and easy to maintain, and prime considerations are flooring, lighting, heating and ventilation. It is worth spending a little more in the first instance rather than have the inconvenience and expense of replacement.

Flooring

It is impossible to be dogmatic about the most suitable type of floor covering in a house, for this depends on a number of variable factors, including the type of disability, the room, the cost, and the means of maintenance. In a home where one person is in a wheelchair, it must be hard wearing (it has to stand up to constant heavy wheeled traffic), easy to propel a wheelchair over, resistant to wheeltracks, and easy to keep clean. Thick pile carpet should be avoided.

An ambulant person, however, whether on crutches or merely unsteady, needs a floor surface which is non slip whether wet or dry, hard wearing and not marked by crutch tips or heavy surgical footwear, and easy to clean and keep clean. Generally speaking, mats on a polished or parquet floor are hazardous for ambulant disabled people; wall-to-wall carpet or vinyl tiles are preferable.

No floor covering is likely to be perfect, but good quality fitted carpet where appropriate, and vinyl flooring (either in sheet or tile form) in passages, kitchen and bathroom, should be satisfactory. Both carpet and vinyl are expensive, but as much of the cost of floor covering lies in the labour involved, it is worth paying more initially to avoid frequent renewal.

Lighting

Adequate lighting in the home is necessary for both safety and efficiency. The placing of individual lights in a room depends partly on the purpose they are to serve – direct lighting or overall illumination – and partly on the general desired effect. Poor lighting leads to strain and fatigue, and may well cause accidents.

During the day, natural daylight is probably sufficient, except in dark corners of rooms and in cupboards, or where especially close work is involved. A disabled person may not be able to take his work to the daylight, and therefore there should be an accessible source of artificial light at hand.

In addition to general lighting for the whole room, it is necessary to have a concentrated source of light over each 'activity zone', whether the writing desk, reading chair, sewing table, or the various busy spots in the kitchen: sink, cooker, preparation area.

Adequate lighting is needed for all jobs, particularly when using a Possum control unit. Possum is described on page 50.

Good artificial lighting needs careful planning, as to both siting and choice of shade and type of bulbs or tubes. Generally speaking, a single lighting fitting in a room is less satisfactory than several arranged in strategic positions. Switches next to doors should be aligned horizontally with door handles, about 90 to 105cm above floor level for wheelchair users. Light switches must be easy to reach. It is usually best to have one switch on the lighting fitting itself, and a second control by the door or bed. A dimmer switch is a useful feature for those who want a low level of light while listening to the radio or television, or while resting.

A variety of switches is available, each requiring a different movement to operate:

a rocker type, which requires a little pressure on a small area
b tip switch, a larger rocker type which is very simple to operate

c pressure switch, which requires only slight pressure and is suitable for those with minimal movement. It can be adapted for use by blowing

d cord ceiling switch (as in a bathroom), which can be fitted with a large ring at the bottom so that it can be operated by an arm movement
e foot or hand pressure switch

f warmth-sensitive switch, which operates as the warmth from any part of the body touches it

In addition, a light switch which operates when a door is opened (as in a refrigerator) can be fitted for use in a pantry or cupboard.

Heating
It is quite likely that the disabled person will require a higher level of heating than other members of the family, particularly if he is unable to take exercise. It is essential, therefore, that each member of the family can exercise some control over his own environment. For handicapped people a temperature of 20°C in living rooms and 16°C in bedrooms, bathrooms, WCs, kitchens and passages is desirable. Some will prefer a higher temperature in the bathroom and WC.

Underfloor heating satisfies these requirements, particularly for those with foot disabilities. Where carpet is laid, however, the efficiency of underfloor heating is reduced, and to compensate for this loss the surface temperature of the floor should be higher than usual.

One disadvantage of electric underfloor heating is that it is relatively inflexible, so adjustment cannot be made rapidly. In any case, supplementary local heaters will probably be required when central heating is installed, either to boost the temperature of the room the disabled person is using, while still keeping the general level acceptable to the rest of the family, or to meet sudden changes in temperature. This may be by means of convector or radiant heaters, though these are apt to cause discomfort to those with catarrh or sinus complaints.

Some central heating radiators have controls which allow the temperature in each room to be individually regulated. A more sophisticated arrangement controlled by a motorised valve and time switch allows particular sections of the house (bedroom, study, bathroom) to be heated during the day. Heater controls must be easy to manipulate, and should not be lower than 53cm above floor level. The preferred minimum is 70cm. For a bedridden person, an additional heating control by the bed is an advantage.

While solid fuel heaters, in particular open fires, are not easy for disabled people to maintain, they are often much appreciated for their companionship and movement. If the rest of the family co-operates in filling coal scuttles, and adequate tongs are available, then a disabled person may get a great deal of pleasure from an open fire. Such a fire is, of course, potentially hazardous, and an adequate fireguard should be used. Obviously someone with difficulties in co-ordination, or with an illness such as epilepsy, should not be left alone with an open fire. Care should be taken that tending the fire does not become a burden or an anxiety to the handicapped person. If structural alterations are feasible, a raised hearth built at a level of 23 to 45cm above the floor makes it easier for those with reach limitations.

Ventilation

In any room used mainly or exclusively by the disabled person, he should be able to control the ventilation by opening or closing the windows. For most disabled (and indeed a number of elderly) people, sash windows present great problems. A casement window, a horizontally sliding window, a fanlight operated by a long lever, or a glass-louvred window or fanlight operated by levers are various solutions. The controls must be accessible (135cm for a chairbound disabled person, 163cm for an ambulant disabled person), and should be easy to manipulate.

A captive sliding stay locked in position with a lever arm overcomes the danger of a window blowing open out of reach. Fixed appliances, such as sinks, or large pieces of furniture, such as tables, should not be located in front of windows, as a disabled person could not reach across them to the window control.

In a kitchen, bathroom or WC some form of extractor can be used. Wind-operated ventilators vary in their performance, but if used wisely are satisfactory. An electric fan is the most effective, and can be fitted to an outside wall or in a window. There are two types of extractor hood which can be fitted over a cooker. One filters the fumes, the other has a duct which transfers smells to the outside. An extractor fan must be suited in performance and size to your needs, and should not be kept on permanently, as it will remove warmth.

Chapter 3
Common-use areas

Shared space must be easily accessible; both the house or flat and the rooms within, doors, outer and inner, passages and porch, must be within the reach and capabilities of the disabled member of the family.

If the entrance to the house is not on the level, it may be necessary to construct a ramp. It must be of the correct dimensions, have a non-slip surface and preferably a safety curb on each side. (See Appendix D for details.) While a ramp is essential to a wheelchair user if there is more than one step, it is not necessarily the best solution for an ambulant person with a stick, crutches or poor co-ordination, who will need special safeguards such as a guard rail and roughening of the surface to prevent slipping. He may find it easier to use steps if they are not too steep, so long as adequate rails and pull-up handles are provided.

The front door must be easy to open and there must be space in the porch or on the landing to manoeuvre a wheelchair if necessary, or with a supporting bar on rails for an ambulant person. A shelf on which to put parcels or a basket when opening the door is a bonus for ambulant people.

Two-way light switches are necessary, both immediately inside the door (within reach of the disabled person on entry and exit), and at the other end of the passage. Passages must be of suitable width (see Appendix D) and may need either a bar at hand height or a protective skirting board. Similarly corners should be protected against wheelchair damage where necessary.

If the handicapped person is ambulant, there should be a pull-up handle beside any step, on the 'good' upside if possible, but on each side if both hands or arms are weak. Door handles are discussed in Chapter 8. The base of doors should be protected by a kickplate.

Flooring in passages should have a non-slip surface (see Chapter 2) and, for

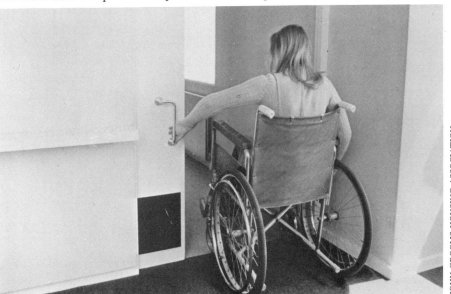

JOHN GROOMS HOUSING ASSOCIATION

the ambulant user, there should if possible be no change of level between passage and room, such as the metal edging to a carpet, which is potentially dangerous. Thick pile carpet should be avoided for wheelchair users and for people with crutches.

Once inside the common-use room, the disabled person should feel he shares it equally with the rest of the family. Any adaptations or alterations should be unobtrusive and in accordance with the general decoration scheme. Most adjustments are those of good design, and will benefit everyone. They include accessibility of electrical and other controls both for heating and lighting, and adequate lighting and ventilation, as discussed in Chapter 2. If it is at all possible, the height of the windows should be such that a wheelchair-bound person or one who finds difficulty in standing can look out; it is tantalising to hear the cries of 'Oh, look at that', and not be able to see what is happening. The lower sill should be about 61cm above floor level. Possibly in a living room one window could be converted to a French window (with a ramp if necessary) allowing both sight of and access to the garden.

The entrances to flats in this John Grooms development are wide and level for wheelchair access, and the doors have easily grasped handles set at a convenient height. There are burglar-proof delivery hatches by the front door so that milk and post can be collected from inside. An intercom allows residents to speak to visitors, and a warning light will alert help in case of emergency. There is an audible alarm outside some flats.

17

In a living room, the room plan is of great importance, but this is very much a matter of individual choice, depending on the number in the family and their social habits. If the disabled person is in a wheelchair he will need much more room than an ambulant person, both for turning the chair and for manoeuvring. A turning space of 1.5m by 1.5m is required, 800 per cent more than the normal ambulant person needs. It is better, therefore, to dispense with any unnecessary furniture.

The disabled person may remain in his wheelchair or sit in an easy chair or on a couch, or possibly on a cushion or 'bean bag' on the floor; this is a matter of individual choice. A good standard or table lamp located next to and controlled from the usual chair is essential. Remote controls for television are desirable but expensive.

In the eating area or dining room, the height of the table and chairs is important. For ambulant people the surface of the dining table should normally be at 70 to 71cm, with chair seats at 43cm, but the chair height may need adjustment. For a wheelchair user, a higher table surface may be preferred, but this would be too high for other users, and the height is very much a matter of preference. It is dependent partly on the height of his chair and the depth of his thighs, but anyone with impaired arm function needs a table as near elbow height as possible. A table which allows knee access only for the wheelchair user (rather than thigh access) is probably best. This means that there must be an unobstructed minimum height of 67cm above floor level.

Children in wheelchairs present a particular problem as their chairs are often too low for them to eat at the same table as the rest of the family. In this case it is best for them either to use a lapboard or to have their own lower table, where other children might have their meals too. Low-level crossbars on dining tables should be avoided in all cases.

Elderly and some other disabled people need an afternoon or evening rest, and for some it is preferable to write or read with their legs up. A couch or divan bed would be a permanent feature in a room, but a folding garden chair gives more scope for dual use. Models with arms, and which incorporate a thin foam rubber covering, are relatively inexpensive and are easy to fold away. They vary considerably, and should be tested for height and stability before buying. To give added comfort, a 10cm foamed polythene cushion can be used on the chair, covered in washable material (with a protective waterproof cover if necessary), or with a cheerful rug. So that full advantage may be taken of the chair, there should be a shelf or low table at its side (there is a good range of cantilevered tables available) and a reading light. If the disabled person is alone in the house, the telephone should be accessible.

The furniture in this living room has been kept to a minimum to allow adequate manoeuvring space for the wheelchair user. The light switches are low enough for her to reach and the coffee table is sturdy.

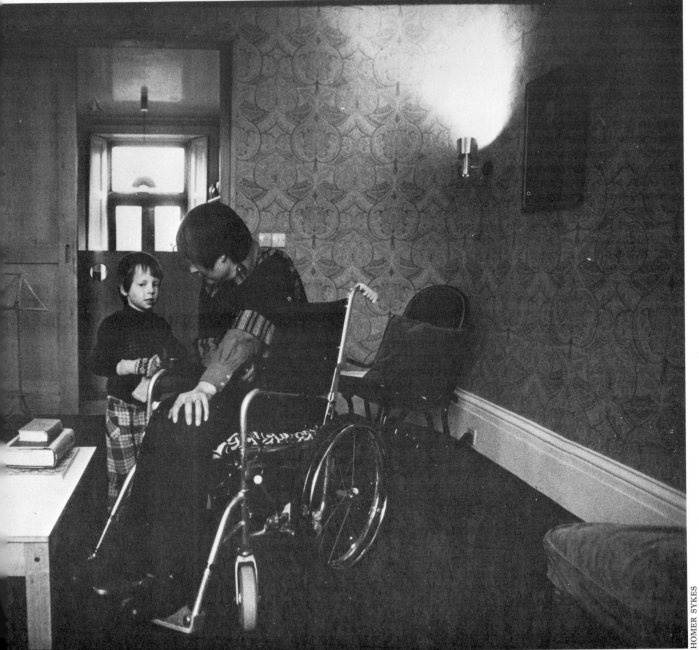

Chapter 4
Kitchens

If the handicapped member of the family is the homekeeper, the kitchen is possibly the most important room in the house. However, any keen cook in the family, whether disabled or able bodied, will want to spend time there. It is therefore essential that the kitchen should be safe and easy to work in and to maintain, and that working in it should be pleasurable.

General arrangement
Here, as elsewhere, access is of the utmost importance, but little or nothing can be done to improve it if the room is unsuitable. Someone in a wheelchair cannot use a kitchen with a threshold step, and it is unlikely to be possible to build a ramp, which would take up a great deal of room (see Appendix D). Sometimes the floor can be built up; another opening can be made; or, as a last resort, the kitchen can be re-sited. Unfortunately any of these alternatives is expensive.

It might be preferable, if space permits, to effect a compromise by transferring some kitchen activities to the dining room, and acknowledging dependence in certain areas. A working counter, with a small split-level electric cooker, could be sited along one wall of the dining area, with a large hatch if possible backing on to the draining board or preparation area on the existing kitchen side. This arrangement would be far from ideal, and would presuppose a fairly constant companion/helper, but it would mean that the disabled person could have some share in the preparation of meals.

The existing floor plan must be carefully studied, first of all in relation to general design principles and second with regard to the specific disability. A logical activity sequence is essential, as it eliminates unnecessary work and movement, thus reducing fatigue and increasing safety.

A window over the sink is not a good idea, as it will be almost impossible for the disabled person to open or close it. There should be an unbroken level working surface between preparation area, sink and cooker, and preferably a heat-proof working surface on the other side of the cooker. If there is a split-level cooker, the oven and hob plates may be separated in the plan, or side by side.

The preferred shape of the room will vary according to the type of disability. A wheelchair user will need sufficient space in which to manoeuvre (see Appendix D), whereas an ambulant person will probably want a more compact space. A wheelchair user may prefer to have the various activity zones spaced along one or at most two sides of the room, while an ambulant person might like a U plan. Other members of the family must also be considered. If other people are likely to be in the kitchen with the wheelchair user, either working or helping, space must be increased so that neither gets in the other's way.

Serving the meal should be made as easy as possible, either by eating in the kitchen (if there is sufficient space) or by having a large hatch opening (at least 120cm wide by 90cm high), linking the preparation area near the cooker with the dining area. This is particularly important for the ambulant user if there is a step between the kitchen and the dining room.

Top right: The usual work sequence in a kitchen. Ideally, storage should be arranged all round the kitchen.
Right: Activity sequences and the arrangement of activity zones. (Taken from Spaces in the home: Kitchens and laundering spaces. *See Appendix E.)*

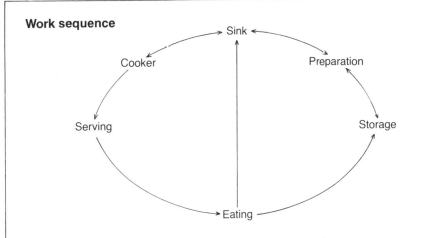

Work sequence

Activity sequences

1 Prepare	**2** Mix	**3** Cook	**4** Serve	**5** Eat	**6** Wash up
Unwrap	Weighing	Baking	Keeping food and dishes hot	Laying table	Disposing of waste
Washing	Measuring	Boiling	Putting food onto dishes or plates	Eating	Stacking
Peeling	Mixing	Frying		Clearing away	Washing
Chopping		Grilling			Drying
Mincing					Putting away
Adding water					

Arrangement of activity zones

1 ⌣ 6	2	3	4	5
Sink	Work surface	Cooker	Work surface or table	Work surface or table
Work surface	Equipment	Work surface	Equipment	Equipment
Equipment	Food	Equipment	Food	Food
Food		Food		
Waste				

Dimensions

Heights and widths, both for preparation and storage, need careful thought, so that so far as possible they are suitable for both able-bodied and disabled people. For a wheelchair user, at least two working heights are necessary; one of these must be provided by a continuous working surface which joins the various activity zones (and which will be used by everyone working in the kitchen), and the other by pull-out boards or lap-boards. A table, if it is the right height (70 to 71cm), may be useful to the wheelchair user, as he can get his legs under it. The sink is likely to be too low if the other activity points are the right height, but its working height can be raised by using a platform in the sink and a plastics bowl for working.

An ambulant person may prefer to sit or stand in the kitchen. If he sits, stools of various heights are useful, so that different activities can be carried out in comfort. If he is much shorter than average, mounting blocks or low steps

with a rail will increase his height without making the kitchen intolerable for other users. For people with poor co-ordination or with instability, a supporting strap is a great help. This must be designed in co-operation with a physio- or occupational therapist.

ILLUSTRATIONS BY JAN CHURCHER

As a guide, the main working surface can be taken as 7.5cm below the elbow when in a normal working position. A number of kitchen activities are less tiring if performed at a lower height: mixing pastry, for example, or beating eggs. If the disabled person can manage only *some* of the cooking, or if he has a condition such as rheumatoid arthritis or multiple sclerosis where he can manage only on 'good' days, then a compromise as to working surface heights might be necessary. In general, however, if the disabled person is the 'working' member in the kitchen, then conditions should be designed with his comfort in mind.

23

Storage

Storage is dependent on both width and height. Various measures can be taken to overcome problems of reaching *down*, but little use can be made by the disabled person of storage space that is too high. This should be given over to stores and equipment that are seldom used. Here is the need for planned dependence.

Various types of kitchen unit and aid can be used:

half-width cupboards
carousels, in corners and on worktops

baskets/shelves on backs of doors
pull-out wire drawers
storage below shelves
vegetable racks on castors
peg board
pull-out and pull-down-fronted drawers
divided vertically

An ambulant person may find difficulty in reaching lower storage, hence vertically divided drawers and back-of-the-door storage are particularly valuable. Where possible, any heavy item of equipment, such as a mixer or blender, should be located at the back of a working surface so that it can be pulled forward rather than lifted. Some food mixers can be fitted onto a swing-out platform which can be pushed away into a cupboard under the worktop when not in use.

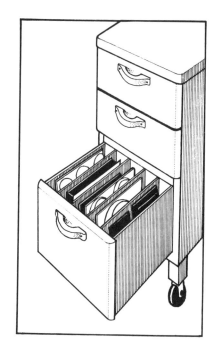

The photographs opposite show various kitchen devices helpful to disabled people. Above left: A pull-out board with cut-out bowl holders gives a secure mixing surface Above right: A carousel fitted in a corner below the worktop makes storage accessible. Below left: Another carousel, here a swing-out basket in a cupboard. Below right: A bank of drawers on wheels provides portable storage for any room.

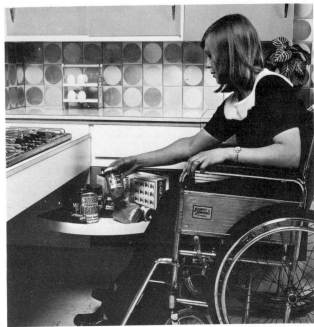

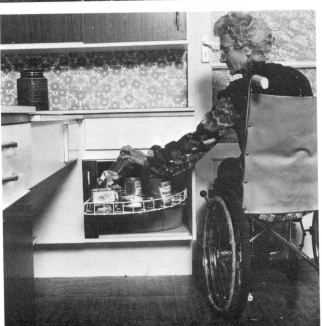

Equipment

The choice of cooker is governed by many factors, including availability, safety and convenience. If supplies of both gas and electricity are available, then the type of disability is important. A partially sighted person, a confused or forgetful one, or someone with poor co-ordination or the use of only one hand, is probably safer with an electric cooker. An 'eye-level' grill is useless to someone in a wheelchair, whose eyes are on quite a different level.

Opinions as to the relative advantages of side-opening and drop-front ovens vary: it is best to try out both. Controls too should be tested, for both accessibility and ease of operation.

Specially brailled controls are available for both gas and electric appliances. Most manufacturers supply on request switch and tap handle additions to make operation easier for those with weak hands. It should be possible to obtain further information and to test out different models of cooker at your local showrooms.

The hob plate should be on a level with the preparation surface, and this dictates the height of the oven unless the cooker is a split-level model. A split-level cooker will, however, diminish working space. The cooker's height can be raised by resting it on a plinth, or individual electric rings can be set into a working surface in a convenient position.

The use of a trolley, with a heat-proof tray at the height of the main-use oven shelf is helpful when dishing up, as is the use of an electrically heated serving tray or trolley.

For those whose mobility is extremely restricted, an electric table cooker (casserole or lidded frying pan) or a portable grill serves the purpose well, though to a limited extent. An electric kettle (with automatic cut-out device) can be fitted to a tilter base to save

lifting. An electric water boiler can be fitted near the sink and filled by a hose from the tap. The water level is visible, and the water actually boils.

The siting and height of a sink are important. A sink is better not located in front of a window; if re-arrangement of the kitchen is possible it is probably most convenient if the sink is against the same wall as, but not immediately in front of, the serving hatch and nearby

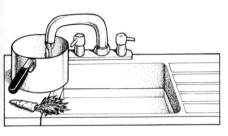
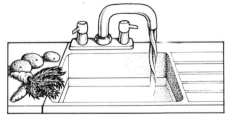

storage. Someone in a wheelchair needs space below the sink for his knees, therefore a shallow model of 12.5 or 15cm is most suitable. If space and money allow, then a double sink, one shallow and one deeper (20 or 22.5cm) is useful. Taps should be raised high enough to allow bowls and saucepans to be filled easily, and the swivel mixer type is the easiest to operate and the least fatiguing for people with weak hands.

To a disabled homekeeper, a refrigerator is one of the most important items of equipment in the kitchen. It enables meals to be planned and stored ahead, and food to be prepared at leisure. Furthermore, storage is well planned and accessible. A small refrigerator can be wall hung, and a larger one mounted on a plinth if it needs to be higher. A combined refrigerator/freezer provides the added facility of longer term storage in the freezing compartment.

A food freezer can be a boon, but it involves considerable work in preparation, and needs careful planning and organisation. It may well prove an added anxiety rather than a labour-saving device, so pros and cons should be carefully considered. Upright models are far easier to use than the chest type, whether the disabled person is ambulant or in a wheelchair. Some handicapped people can do the stationary jobs such as preparing and listing home-grown fruit and vegetables for the food freezer that an able-bodied person might not have time for.

A disabled housewife is likely to want comparatively little additional kitchen equipment, indeed it is probable that she may require fewer appliances, for she will be more discriminating. There are, however, some 'optional extras' in the kitchen, such as a waste disposal unit or dishwasher, which may be useful to a disabled person. As with all additional equipment, each piece should be closely examined to see whether it will really be valuable. If you cannot afford it, and it is not *really* essential, put it out of your mind. Quite apart from the question of expense, however, you should see whether it will fit into the available space, or reduce storage and cramp up other space. Make sure the disabled person can operate it easily, that it is easy to keep clean, and really does save time and effort. Check also that the disabled person will like using it. (Many families buy their mother an expensive piece of sophisticated equipment that is a burden to her. Instead of its being time- and labour-saving and a pleasure to use, she views it with fear and apprehension.) Think well before buying.

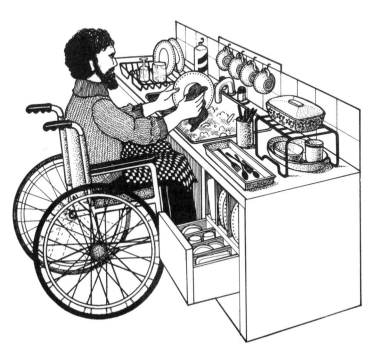

Flooring, lighting and ventilation

Flooring, lighting and ventilation are discussed in detail in Chapter 2. Flooring in the kitchen must be hard wearing and easy to maintain, and should be resistant to grease and acids. Most important, it should be non slip when wet; however careful one is, water is often spilt in the kitchen, and crutch tips and surgical shoes are apt to skid.

Lighting in the kitchen should be placed above work centres and should give a pleasant and efficient light without glare. A good place for a light over a working surface is underneath a wall cupboard, using a shaving light with a press-button switch. It is useful to have duplicate switches for the main light if there are two doors, so that the light can be easily controlled.

Ventilation in the kitchen should be simple and efficient, and may well mean more than just a window, which can be difficult or impossible for a disabled person to manipulate. The wooden upper half of the back door can be replaced by a louvred glass window, which gives extra light as well as ventilation, or it can be converted into a 'stable door', in which the top half can be opened separately. (A milk bottle holder could be attached to it, to save an outside journey.) An extractor hood can be placed above the cooker, or an electric extractor fan fitted in the window or an outside wall.

Safety

Safety considerations are particularly important in the kitchen, where a disabled person is likely to be vulnerable to risks because of lack of balance or co-ordination, poor sight or hearing, slow reaction or movement, and fatigue. All the usual precautions should be taken and a small, easily operated fire extinguisher is really essential, also a first aid box. (Safety is discussed in detail in Chapter 7.)

Fatigue is something that can be guarded against, and there should not only be adequate seating (by means of stools of various heights) for the ambulant person, but also active encouragement for periodic 'time off'. This should be in a corner of the kitchen with the provision of an easy chair, magazines and cookery books, pleasant lighting, and a timer so that the cook can relax without guilt.

Reference for the drawings in this chapter was taken from Kitchen sense for disabled or elderly people, *illustrated by Brenda Naylor (see Appendix E).*

Chapter 5
Bathrooms and WCs

For the convenience of the handicapped person, it is desirable to have the bathroom and WC situated as close to his bedroom as possible: indeed, it may lead directly from the bedroom with a second door giving access from a passage. However, it should be remembered that some disabled people spend a long time bathing or using the WC, and therefore if it is not possible to have two WCs, the bathroom and WC should be separate. The door of both bathroom and WC should open outwards, or be of a sliding type. It should have a lock or bolt which can be opened from outside in an emergency.

This wheelchair user's bathroom has a wide doorway for easy access, an open area under the washbasin, and a useful swing-out mirror on the door of the cabinet.

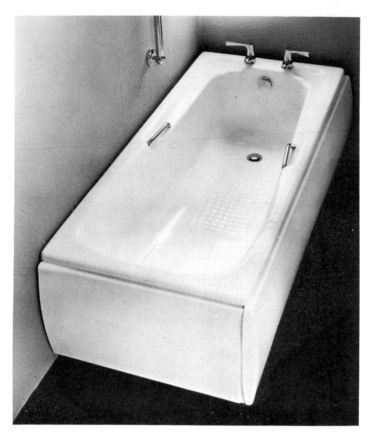

A bath with a slip-resistant finish for showering, metal hand grips and lever taps is advisable for handicapped people. From Nicholls & Clarke

Space

An ambulant disabled person may need additional space in the bathroom, so that he can get into and out of the bath easily. In most cases, there should be a platform at the end of the bath to which transfer can be made from a stool or chair, and a similar arrangement may also be suitable for a wheelchair user.

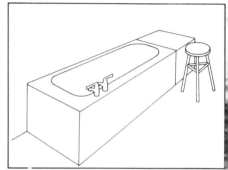

Other ambulant users may need more space beyond the platform, or a deeper platform, so that they can pull themselves out of the bath using their elbows and shoulders and then transfer to a chair or stool.

Any bath seat should be well away from the taps. Transfer from chair to bath may be made by use of a sliding board, hoist or other mechanical means. A stable seat should be provided for all ambulant users.

Washbasins

If possible, a washbasin should be provided in the disabled person's bedroom. For an ambulant disabled person the preferred rim height is 91cm, and the basin can be either wall hung or fitted in a vanitory unit. If the user is in a wheelchair, the rim height should be

80cm, and space in front must be allowed for the chair. A special washbasin has been designed for spastics and people with unco-ordinated movement, with an anti-splash rim. Taps should be accessible and easy to operate. A lever type is most suitable.

A washbasin with an open area underneath is the most convenient for a wheelchair user, and lever taps are the easiest type to operate. Washbasin and taps from Nicholls & Clarke

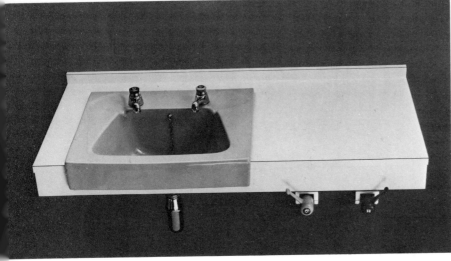

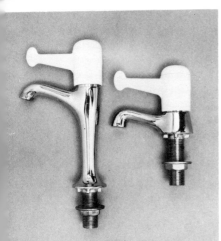

WCs

Ambulant disabled people should not need extra space in a WC, so a room measuring 80cm wide by 150cm deep should be satisfactory. A wheelchair user should have space to manoeuvre his chair, but in some smaller rooms this may not be possible. If he can transfer to the WC by taking a few steps, he should be able to make do with the same space as ambulant users. Others must transfer from wheelchair to WC seat, frontwards or laterally, and in many cases must be assisted.

Transfer is far easier if the WC pan is parallel with the face of the door. If the wheelchair user does not need help, a room measuring 170cm by 140cm is adequate for lateral transfer and will allow a wheelchair to be turned.

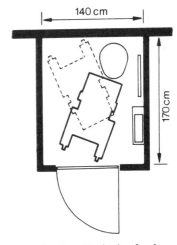

Diagram taken from Designing for the disabled *by Selwyn Goldsmith*

If he needs assistance, the room must be large enough to accommodate WC pan, wheelchair and helper, or hoist and helper. In this case it should measure at least 180cm by 110cm, to enable the

31

disabled person to make an assisted frontal oblique transfer. If there is a second WC for the use of the rest of the family, it need not be large enough to accommodate a wheelchair.

Most disabled people, and many who are comparatively able bodied, also need support in the form of rails or handles.

and the disabled person must be consulted here. They can be either attached to the walls, or set around the seat and fixed to the floor. Some badly disabled people need additional help by means of a mechanical hoist, and these aids are discussed in Chapter 8. If there is room in a separate WC, a small washbasin should be placed where it can be reached by the disabled user.

Showers

While a shower is easier for most people, many handicapped people much prefer bathing, as it is therapeutic. However, for those who cannot easily or independently manage bathing, a shower is a satisfactory (although sometimes expensive) alternative. It may be possible to incorporate a shower unit in the bathroom (either in the bath or in a separate cabinet), or it may be necessary to construct a separate room (perhaps incorporating a WC).

For ease of operation, the floor of a shower should be on the same level as the floor outside, with no step up for the user. The shower can have rails at the sides and may incorporate a small fixed or sliding bench or seat. Alternatively, a wheelchair user may transfer to a sani-chair which can be pushed under the shower. For many disabled people, and particularly those with poor sensation, a thermostatic control is important.

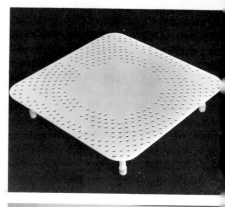

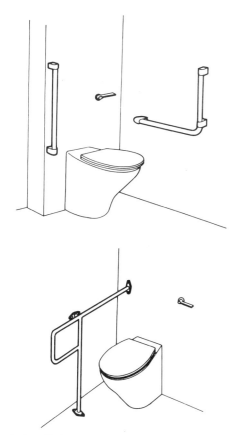

WC rails from Modric Limbar range by G S Allgood (top) and Carters (J & A) Ltd

These are used both to guide and stabilise the body, and as a means by which to pull upright. It is impossible to be dogmatic about their size or placing,

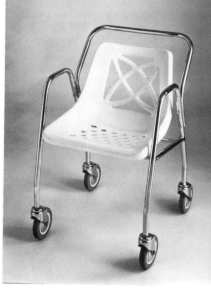

Top: A raised grating placed in a shower will bring it up to the level of the bathroom floor for easy access by disabled people. Above: For taking a shower, a wheelchair user can transfer to a wheeled shower chair, in which he can be pushed into the cabinet.

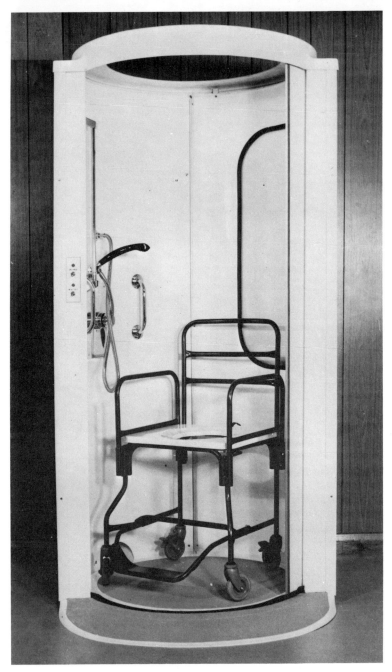

Bidets

A bidet is a useful addition, particularly for a non-ambulant disabled person who has difficulty in washing the crutch area. There is one available which is higher than normal and which can be used in an ordinary sitting position rather than sitting astride.

Heating

Bathrooms, shower rooms and WCs should always be adequately heated. The disabled person will be slow, and needs warm surroundings. A heated towel rail is an excellent source of extra warmth, and ensures warm dry towels at all times. In a combined bathroom and WC it can well be placed above the cistern.

Medicines

All drugs and medicines should be kept in a locked cabinet, preferably one fitted with a child-proof catch which will deter confused and unreliable people as well as children. It should not be fixed to the wall above a washbasin where dropped bottles could smash. A special shelf or cupboard may be needed for the use of the disabled person, and where supplies such as incontinence pads, 'wet wipes' and dressings can be kept.

Special bathing and sanitary aids and equipment are described in Chapter 8.

The Chiltern shower unit has been designed with the handicapped in mind, but can also be used without adaptation by able-bodied people. The disabled person is wheeled on a shower chair up a short ramp into the cabinet. He then closes the curved sliding door, in which there is a large access panel. The shower unit is thermostatically controlled for extra safety, and there are hand grips. By Chiltern Medical Developments (Equipment)

Chapter 6
Special-purpose rooms

Although most accommodation in the home will be shared by the whole family, there are certain rooms which are special to the disabled person and which should be planned with particular care. The disabled person's bedroom and study (if he has one) will probably be designed expressly for that person, unless it is a shared bedroom. A playroom for a disabled child may be designed with him in mind, but it serves its purpose better if it aims at maximum participation by the child's own brothers and sisters, and by his able-bodied friends.

The disabled person's need for privacy is important. Obviously family life implies sharing and co-operation, and this is a good thing. But for a disabled person, who has probably had to undergo periods in hospital and attendant 'fussing' by his family, a quiet retreat of his own is essential. This may be merely a corner of a shared bedroom, but it should be the owner's private domain. To ensure such privacy it is necessary to provide special aids to independence: easy access, adequate storage, control of lighting, heating and ventilation, possibly some form of alarm or call system, preferably telephone or intercom, toilet facilities or easy access to a shared WC, and – in cases of severe disablement – a hoist.

Bedrooms

For a bedroom it is essential to have a bed which is comfortable, easy to get into and out of, easy to make, of a temperature controllable by the occupant, and sited so that the disabled person has accessible and adequate bedside storage for books, spectacles, medicines, water, tissues and so on. If the handicapped person spends long periods in bed, then its appearance is particularly important, as a hospital atmosphere must be avoided. A continental quilt is comfortable and practical, and a matching cover, sheet and pillowcases in a minimum-care terylene and cotton mixture, look gay and uninstitutional. If a cradle over the legs is necessary, the upper bed clothes (top sheet and blankets, or continental quilt and cover) must be double-bed size.

The type of mattress is important, and advice on this should be available from a doctor, physio- or occupational therapist or from a community (district) nurse, if she visits. Generally speaking, a firm mattress is preferable, possibly with fracture boards above or below the wire mattress. Foam rubber mattresses do not need to be turned, and may be protected from soiling by a plastic cover. For those who cannot turn themselves in bed, various types of anti-pressure material are available, such as ripple mattresses or sheepskin. The type of bed is something which should be discussed with a doctor or therapist.

The preferred height of the bed will again depend on the disability. For most arthritics and those with a heart condition, a height of 45 to 50cm entails the least effort on getting up and returning to bed; this is particularly important if the disabled person needs to go to the lavatory during the night. (If the WC is not nearby, a commode, or for men a bottle urinal, is useful.) A higher bed is also easier to make, particularly if a continental quilt and fitted sheets are used. For a handicapped person in a wheelchair, transfer is easier if the bed is the same height as the wheelchair seat (with cushion).

Warmth in bed is something very individual; some disabled people need considerable additional heat, while others are liable to throw off a continental quilt or blankets as the night

Anyone who spends long periods in bed needs an adequate bedside table. This mobile locker by Paramount has a pull-out tray.

progresses. Light electric overblankets are easily controlled and do not add a lot of weight. An electric heating pad takes the place of a hot water bottle, and is both safer and easier to control.

A bedside table with a drawer, or built-in shelves if the head of the bed is in an alcove or against the wall, will ensure that wants are at hand. If the disabled person spends much time in bed, or in a wheelchair or easy chair in the bedroom, it will be necessary to provide a table for meals, reading and writing, and this could be part of a bedside locker. This is a matter of individual choice but the cantilevered types are stable and manoeuvrable, and are reasonably easy to adjust. The old type of bed table which slides over the bed inhibits movement and is very constricting, and cannot be used if there is any type of cradle over the legs.

If the bedroom is on the ground floor, access provides few problems, assuming that passages and doorways are of

suitable width for a wheelchair user (see Appendix D). For an upper floor bedroom, stairs are negotiable by most ambulant people if a rail is provided on each side. Although this is not an ideal arrangement, it works well so long as the disabled person does not have to go up and down frequently; a downstairs WC and, for some people, a place to rest are essential. Many elderly and some ambulant disabled people tire easily and need to rest during the day on a couch,

day bed or long garden chair. For wheelchair users there is one model which reclines fully, thus doing away with the need to transfer to a bed or couch. For some it is better and less tiring to read, work or watch television with their legs up, and a folding garden chair with arms and light foam cushions takes up little space. The cushions can be covered in a suitable washable material and if necessary the mattress can be protected by a waterproof cover.

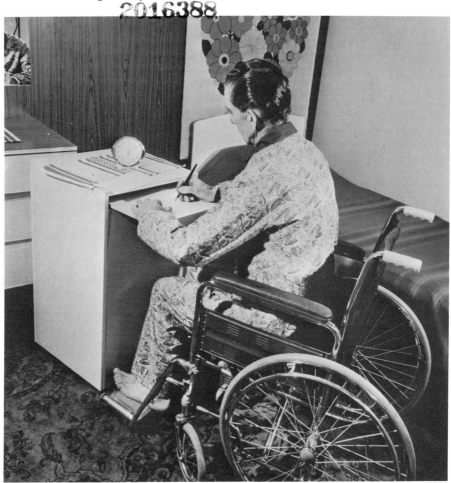

35

Storage

Storage space depends very much on the use to which the room is put, whether it is shared, and whether the disabled person has other space of his own, such as a study or workroom. If he virtually lives in the room, largely in bed and dependent on others, storage heights are less critical for those things which others will put away. However, he needs to see his belongings and to identify with them. It is all the more important in such a case that he has sufficient easily accessible storage for all his needs, medicines, washing kit (and make-up for a woman), reading and writing things, radio and television, and any controls and essential aids such as some form of communication (alarm system, call button, telephone or Possum). Anyone who has been in hospital knows how frustrating most bedside lockers are: not capacious enough, intractable in movement and often unsteady, liable to lose vital possessions from the top, and confused within.

For someone to whom bed is not a way of life, bedside storage is not essential: a bedside table or shelf with room for books, spectacles, radio and glass of water is sufficient. For an ambulant disabled person or a reasonably independent wheelchair user, there must be storage for clothes, toilet things (including any special dressings needed) and personal possessions. If the room doubles as a study or playroom, books, papers or toys must also be considered.

For clothes, shelves with pull-out baskets are probably easier than drawers. Hanging rails for a wheelchair user should not be higher than 145cm above floor level. A long mirror is an asset, for both men and women.

For a child, a bedroom will probably be shared with a brother or sister. Privacy and storage can be combined by the use of back-to-back cupboards or, better still, by units which open on alternate sides, giving each occupant a share of storage and pin-up space. With this type of cupboard heights can be adjusted so that the storage is easily accessible to the handicapped child.

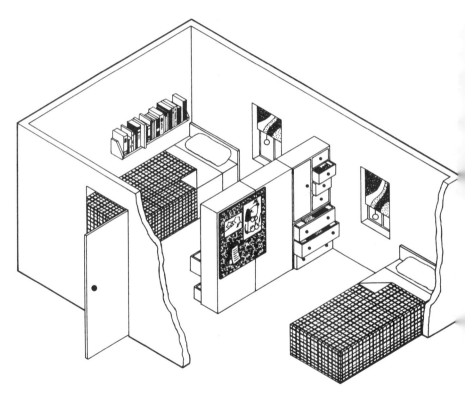

This wardrobe by Paramount has a low rail within reach of wheelchair users.

Controls and services

Controls should be accessible when the user is both in and out of bed, and this applies particularly to lighting and communication signals. There must be an accessible light switch by the door and another at the side of the bed. (Controls are discussed in detail in Chapter 8.)

Lighting should be pleasant and adequate for the type of activity to be carried on. The room is likely to have much more intensive use than most bedrooms, and provision must be made for reading in bed, possibly also at a desk or table, and for general social purposes.

Not only should there be alternative sources of light — at bedside, dressing table, desk and chair — but some form of dimmer switch is also useful. (Lighting is discussed in detail in Chapter 2.)

Even if the house is centrally heated, it may be necessary to provide additional heat, for some handicapped people are particularly susceptible to cold. In addition to specific bed heating (electric blanket or warming pad), it may be possible to modify the central heating system so as to provide heat as and when it is needed in a particular section of the house (bedroom, study, bathroom). If a separate source of heating is provided, it must be both safe (no unguarded fires) and easily controllable, by a switch within reach. (Heating is discussed in detail in Chapter 2.)

Ventilation is very important, and if the bedroom is constantly occupied some form of deodorant may be required. An extractor fan ensures a change of air but must be of the right capacity for the size of the room. A casement window is easier to open than a sash window, and a fanlight or louvred glass window with a lever easier still. Even though many disabled people (especially older ones) dread draughts, fresh air should not be excluded on this account. (Ventilation is discussed in detail in Chapter 2.)

Communication

A disabled person should be able to count on support when he needs it, and therefore some form of communication should be available in the bedroom. This may take the form of a bell, an intercom (a children's alarm system), a telephone, or a Possum control, depending on the disabled person's circumstances and capabilities. (Communication is discussed in detail in Chapter 8.)

Hoists

It may be necessary to install a hoist, either to get into bed or to transfer from bedroom to bathroom or WC. Expert advice should be sought from a therapist on the type of hoist required and on installation, and ideally different types should be tried out. (Hoists are discussed in detail in Chapter 8.)

Study/workroom

A study/workroom may be a separate room or a corner of the bedroom. Again privacy is important: it should be the occupant's own particular domain, whether it is for homework, writing, business accounts or household bills, sewing or hobbies. There are few requirements peculiar to a disabled person other than adequate heating and lighting and suitable storage. Again, it must be accessible, have some means of communication, and be sited reasonably near toilet facilities.

Many disabled people will consider working at home rather than tackle all the problems (transport, access, etc) associated with outside employment. In such cases particular care should be taken with the design of the room, which may need to include a typewriter and telephone, sewing machine, drawing board, work table or desk.

Chapter 7
Safety

Safety in the home is a matter of concern to *everyone* for there are far too many avoidable cases of accident and injury. Much of the prevention is based on good functional design and the remainder on common sense.

The elderly and many other disabled people are particularly prone to accidents when they are overtired: they are often unwilling to rest because of pride. Where possible, they should sit to do jobs, and should avoid starting something which cannot be interrupted for a half-way rest. They should learn not to be too proud to accept help – planned dependence is a necessary part of disablement. Fatigue is probably the most common cause of falls and other accidents, both in the home and in the garden, associated with any other of the bad practices discussed below. Other causes which encourage falls are poor lighting, clutter, slippery and uneven flooring, spilt water or grease, worn linoleum, loose mats, trailing flex, badly placed controls and physical disabilities. A handicapped person should have some form of alarm so that he can summon help in case of accident or emergency.

Fatigue
The ambulant disabled person should have ample opportunity for rest, particularly in the kitchen. Disablement means one is slower at most things; it may also involve pain, and it is important not to feel 'driven' when doing a job. A time schedule with forward planning means one can prepare a meal in stages, and not have a frenzied rush when the family comes home.

Lighting
Lighting should always be considered in relation to the use of the space in which it is employed. Lighting in passages and on stairs is intended to show up steps and other hazards – it should not be just an economical low-voltage arrangement which invites errors. In a kitchen, a study or a bedroom, lighting should be placed in relation to activity centres, such as the sink or cooker, the desk or the dressing table. There should be adequate and accessible controls in each case, with two-way switches – at entrances, passages and stairs – where necessary. (Lighting is discussed in detail in Chapter 2.)

Clutter
All members of the household should be taught to clear up their activities as they go – whether it is dirty dishes in the kitchen, discarded clothes in a teenager's room or toys throughout the house. One way of encouraging reasonable tidiness is the provision of adequate and accessible storage: easy-to-reach cupboards in the kitchen, hanging space and dirty clothes bags in the bedroom, toy boxes (made from covered cartons) or bags, shelves for books, and so on.

Flooring
Obviously the state of the flooring throughout the house is an important factor, whether it be the covering, the finish or the surface. From the point of view of the disabled person, the type of floor covering must be suited to his individual needs. For an ambulant person (whether disabled or not) *any* floor surface which is slippery – either because of misplaced polishing, or as a result of water or grease – is extremely dangerous, more so if he uses crutches. Surfaces can be perilous if the covering is worn (linoleum or carpet with holes or bare patches), especially on the stairs; if the boards themselves are cracked or uneven; or if there are loose rugs or mats.

which slip or trip the unsteady walker or the crutch-user. (Flooring is discussed in detail in Chapter 2.)

Other hazards

These are often the result of poor design, such as badly sited power points where the user has to bend or reach into an inaccessible corner. Power points should be at worktop height (approximately 70 to 71cm); controls on heating devices should be on the upper surface, not at ground level; ignition devices on central heating units should be accessible (some are so low one has to sit on the floor to reach them!); and flex should never be allowed to trail over the floor. If the flex for a lamp or fire is too long, it should be folded together and secured by a rubber band, or with tape.

Stairs

Stairs are definitely hazardous for the elderly or ambulant disabled person, and a firm rail should be provided on each side. They should be well lit, and the floor covering should be unworn. If the disabled person is confused, visually handicapped, unstable, epileptic or mentally handicapped, it may be wise to have a barrier at the stair head.

Furniture

For the visually handicapped, furniture that is unstable or has sharp corners should be avoided if there is a danger of the disabled person's bumping into it. 'Occasional' pieces of furniture which serve little useful purpose are likely to present dangerous obstacles to a disabled person. For those who are lame or frail, tables and chairs are almost certainly used as aids in sitting down and getting up, and they need to be reasonably robust and stable. Many disabled people will have experienced the horrors of the tilting theatre seat or the one-legged table.

Poisoning

All the usual precautions should be taken here, as in any household. It is unrealistic to suggest that all medicines should be kept in a locked cabinet if the disabled person is on drugs which must be taken at regular intervals. However, if there are children in the house, or if the patient is confused or unreliable, drugs *must* be kept under lock and key, or in a child-proof cabinet. Special attention is necessary if there is a visually handicapped person in the household who may rely on the shape of a bottle to denote its contents.

Fire

This is probably the most dreaded risk in the home, although falls are more common with elderly or disabled people, and probably more dangerous. The important safety measure here is prevention, first by common sense: careful placing of tea towel racks, fire guards always in front of open fires, and so on, and avoidance of potentially hazardous activities such as deep fat frying or smoking in the kitchen or bedroom. There should be at least one hand-operated fire extinguisher on each floor, as well as in the kitchen, easily accessible and understood by all members of the family. If the disabled person is completely immobile, some means of calling assistance, such as an adapted telephone or an alarm system, should be available.

Electricity

Any electrical work should be done by an expert, rather than by a friendly amateur. The local Electricity Board has a list of qualified electricians who are on the roll of the National Inspection Council for Electrical Installation Contracting (NICEIC). Make sure the circuit is not overloaded by using too many plugs in the same socket outlet; consider the possibility of additional, more conveniently placed, points. Appliances should be serviced at reasonable intervals. This applies particularly to electric blankets.

Gas

Gas water heaters must be fitted with flues and need servicing at six-monthly intervals. A flueless sink water heater is intended to give only small quantities of water at the sink.

First aid

As in a car, it is a sensible precaution to keep a first aid box in an accessible place in the home – probably in the kitchen, as this is where most minor accidents occur. So far as possible the box should be damp proof, child proof, and should contain as basics:

strip plasters of assorted sizes
bandages of assorted sizes
scissors
cotton wool
gauze dressings
assorted safety pins
bottle of antiseptic
bottle of aspirin or paracetamol

Medical authorities recommend that burns and scalds should be covered with gauze and, if severe, seen by a doctor. Indeed, if in doubt with *any* injury, it is better to have it seen to professionally, rather than trying to cope at home with inadequate means.

Chapter 8
Special equipment and alterations

There are some pieces of equipment which are extremely important to a handicapped person, and which may make all the difference between dependence and independence. All the equipment mentioned below should be fully discussed with both the handicapped person himself and an appropriate adviser: doctor, physio- or occupational therapist. It should also be thoroughly tested by the handicapped person, in circumstances as similar as possible to those at home. (Quite a small variation may make all the difference to comfort or even feasibility.) When it comes to cost, financial help *may* be available from the National Health Service or local social services. Again this should be discussed with a doctor or therapist.

Lifts

One of the most useful pieces of special equipment (and also one of the most expensive) is some form of personal lift to overcome the barrier of stairs. Various types of small domestic lift exist, including a stair seat (which can be used either sitting or standing but only on straight stairs); a vertical seat (which can be used between different levels where the stairs are not straight); a personal lift and a home lift, both of which accept a wheelchair.

The simplest of these is the stair seat, which is a self-contained unit and involves no structural alterations. It is particularly suitable for ambulant disabled people who find stairs painful and difficult (both going up and, possibly even more so, coming down). The stair seat occupies only half the width of the stairs and thus allows other people plenty of space to walk up and down beside it.

Stair seat by Wessex Medical Equipment

The vertical seat takes up more room, as it uses a space of approximately 53cm by 75cm on both ground and first floors. This seat lift takes the disabled person from the ground floor to the first floor through a trap door in the ceiling which closes automatically as the lift descends.

In both these types, the disabled person must transfer to the lift seat, and this may not always be easy for someone in a wheelchair. The following two types of lift accept a wheelchair and can be installed if more space is available.

The personal lift, comparatively recently produced, consists of an open platform with a safety stop-rail on to which the chair runs, or alternatively a smaller platform on which a person can stand. It is worked by hand, either by the disabled person himself or by a helper, and the platform ascends through a trap door to the room above. Its small size means it can be installed in the corner of a room.

The home lift is similar in design to a conventional lift, except that it is only powerful enough to lift one person and wheelchair at a time. This model is entirely enclosed, unlike the other lifts described above. This may or may not be appreciated by the disabled person, who may feel either safer or more claustrophobic – again a question of personal preference.

The chair seat is the only type where the disabled person can be accompanied, in this case by someone walking up the stairs beside him as the seat ascends. All the lifts discussed can be operated by either the disabled person or a helper.

Vertical seat by Wessex Medical Equipment

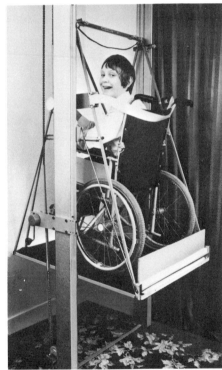

Personal lift by Terry Personal Lifts

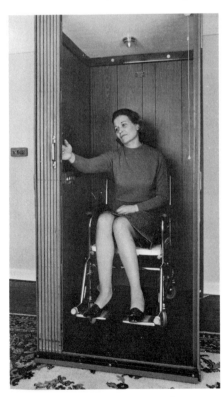

Home lift by Wessex Medical Equipment

Hoists

Broadly speaking, there are three types
of hoist, two of which are manually
operated, the other electrically powered.
The choice of slings is extremely
important.

The mobile hoist is operated by a
helper and transfers a severely disabled
person from chair to bed, from bed or
chair to commode or WC, and in and out
of the bath. It is sometimes necessary to
carry out adaptations, particularly in a
bathroom, to give sufficient manoeuvring
space. If a hoist is needed only for
getting in and out of the bath, a floor-
mounted model may do (see page 45).

The powered hoist is a permanent
installation and comprises a short or
long track, straight or curved, with
lifting equipment. The track may run
from bedroom to bathroom and/or WC,
and operation is normally undertaken by
someone other than the disabled person.
However, in certain cases it is possible
for the user himself to operate the hoist.

The assembly of the manually
operated car hoist is mounted on the
roof of the car, and is permanently fixed
in position by steel clamps. It is
attendant operated.

*This hydraulic car hoist can be mounted on
the roof of most cars and is permanently fixed
in position. By S Burvill & Son*

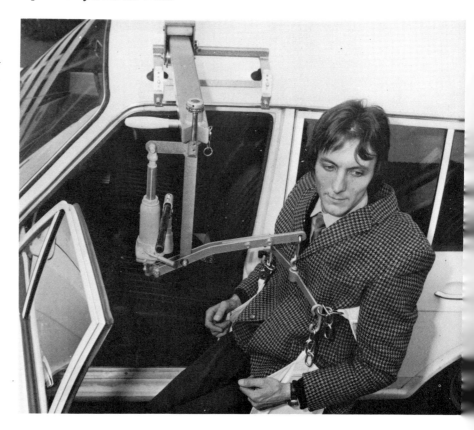

The Wessex range of slings and harnesses is powered by a hoist and traversing motor, which can be attached to either a portable or a permanent track. Below left: A handicapped man in a hammock sling fitted to a Twyford portable track transfers from his wheelchair into bed. Below right: A fixed track running from bedroom to bathroom enables this disabled man to get into the bath without help. Made by Wessex Medical Equipment

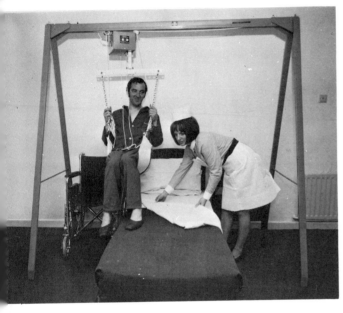

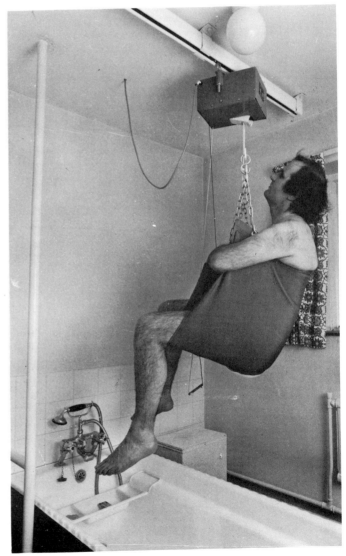

Bathing and sanitary aids

For many types of physical disablement, beginning or ending the day with a warm bath makes a tremendous difference, and any aid which makes this possible is worth investigating. Some of these are not only expensive but involve additional space, as they are specially designed for disabled people and are unsuitable for others.

These include a sitting bath, where the handicapped person transfers from wheelchair to bath seat, then closes the self-sealing door and fills the bath. After the water has been drained off, the door can be opened.

The shower bath unit is designed on similar lines, except that with this model the disabled person transfers from his chair to a movable seat which swings round, and transfer is then made to the fixed seat in the shower unit.

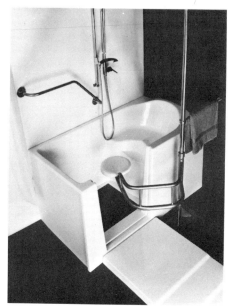

With the Cleveland shower bath unit by Armitage Shanks, the disabled person transfers onto a seat which swivels round into the tub. He then slides onto the seat in the bath, slots in the door and turns on the shower unit.

In both these units, the disabled person must have fairly strong arms, as the transfers involve a certain amount of agility.

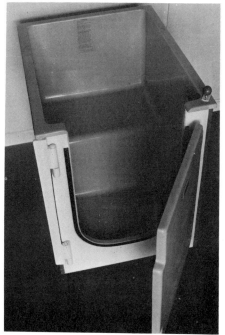

The Mermaid sitting bath unit by Medic-Bath will suit any handicapped person who has difficulty in climbing into and out of a standard bath. Once he has transferred to the seat in the tub, he closes the self-sealing door and fills the bath to waist height.

There are various designs of bath with a built-in seat for handicapped people. This model from Nicholls & Clarke has hand grips

Bath liners, made from warm-feeling, slip-resistant plastic, raise the level of the floor of a bath and can be removed after use. The standard bath is thus available for the rest of the household.

Some bath lifts are designed to be operated either by the disabled person himself or by a helper. The equipment would take up a certain amount of floor space (it is mounted on a pillar bolted to the floor), and this is most important when considering the movement of a wheelchair. However, it would still allow the use of the bathroom by other people.

Above: Plastic bath liners are available in various sizes; some raise the level to make a shallow bath, others enable the disabled person to sit. They can be removed after use, leaving the standard bath free. From Nicholls & Clarke

Left: The Autolift by Mecanaids is a bath lift mounted on a pillar bolted to the floor. It can be operated either by the disabled person himself or by a helper.

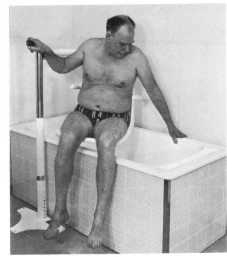

Above: A bath board enables a disabled person to transfer more easily into a standard bath.
Right: A bath seat can be used by a handicapped person in a standard bath.

45

There are also various types of WC rail and WC seat. The WC rails can be free standing or fixed, but do not impede the use of the WC by able-bodied people.

The different types of WC seat can be removed after use, and are available in a range of heights. Made of plastic, they are light and durable and can be stored to one side of the WC or hung on a coat hook behind the door.

A warm-water bidet incorporated in an ordinary WC pan means that a severely handicapped person can be independent in his personal needs. After using the WC in the normal way, the user presses a foot or hand button, which brings a warm-water douche into operation. This is followed by a warm air flow, the whole cleansing operation taking two minutes.

Commodes and sani-chairs can be of use to a disabled person. In domestic situations a chair-commode, in the bedroom or living room, is most useful. Various types of pan are available: the plastic or stainless steel type, with lid and carrying handle, are the most practical. A sani-chair on wheels, to which a bed-ridden or wheelchair-bound person can be transferred *outside* the WC before being wheeled inside, will often solve the problem of a space too restricted to permit transfer within the room. A chemical WC may be useful for a disabled person who has difficulty in emptying a commode pan and no helper to do it for him.

Plastic WC seats, which raise the level of a standard WC pan, can be removed after use by the disabled person. From Carters (J & A) Ltd

The Medic-Loo by Medic-Bath incorporates a warm-water bidet and warm air flow in an ordinary WC pan, so giving even severely handicapped people independence in their personal needs. It can be operated by either a foot button or a hand switch.

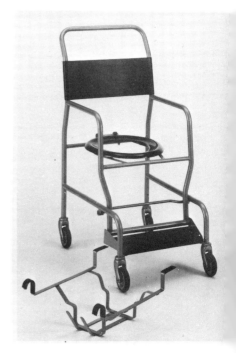

Where space is restricted in a WC, a wheelchair user can transfer onto a sani-chair outside the room and then be wheeled inside. From F Llewellyn & Co

Handles

Generally speaking, a lever type or pull handle is the easiest to operate, and a small smooth knob type the most difficult to manipulate. Door handles should not be higher than 107cm above floor level, but for wheelchair users a height of 90 to 100cm is preferable.

Clearance between handle and door is important, especially for those with deformed or stiff hands, and for those who are ill co-ordinated. A moulded lever handle which fits the hand comfortably and can be gripped securely is suitable for most people, but for wheelchair users it may need to be augmented by a pull handle or horizontal rail, to enable the user to pull the door closed as he passes through.

In general sliding doors, although space saving, are less easy for a disabled person to operate. For cupboards, magnetic catches and 'Tutch' latches (which operate with a gentle push) make doors easier to open.

Lever handles of the type shown here are the easiest for a disabled person to operate. From Nicholls & Clarke

These handles from the Modric Limbar range by G S Allgood are particularly suitable for disabled and ill co-ordinated people.

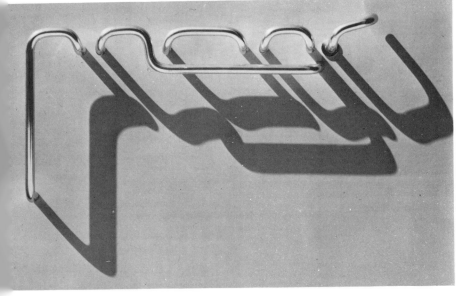

Transport

Wheelchairs, for both indoors and out, are a medical requirement and are not appropriate to this book. Outdoor electric wheelchairs, however, make a tremendous difference to independence, for they give a wide range of mobility. They require a normal domestic power outlet for recharging, and can cover up to twelve miles a day, at a maximum speed of four miles an hour.

Ramps

In most cases, where space allows, a ramp should be permanently installed. In others, however, it may be more convenient to have a portable ramp. (See Appendix D.) Portable ramps can only be used to cover one or two steps.

Above left: The Batricar electric wheelchair by Braune of Stroud can climb a 10cm kerb. It can be driven with one hand only.
Left: An automatic control on a garage door is an asset for a handicapped person. Doors and controls by P C Henderson
Above right: These portable aluminium ramps have rubber pads at each end for extra grip. They fold in half for transfer and storage. By Simcross Services
Right: This movable ramp by Swirl is designed on a module for increased flexibility. The surface is non slip, the edges are raised, and hand rails are available.

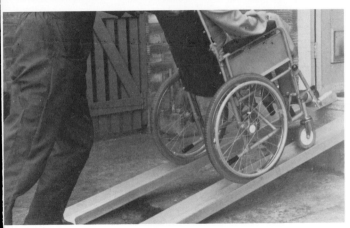

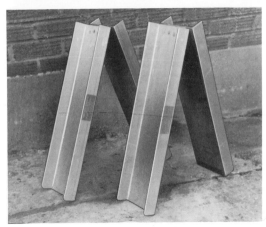

Controls

All forms of control should be both accessible and operable, and this is influenced by both height and siting. Accessibility will depend partly on whether the user is ambulant or in a wheelchair. This applies too with socket outlets for lighting, heating or television; in general, a socket outlet should be at elbow height. In many gas and electric heaters, the controls are situated at the bottom or at the side. In an increasing number, however, the controls are situated on the top of the appliance.

Make sure that the markings on the control are easy to read and understand. It may be necessary to augment them by a spot of paint or nail varnish. (For blind or partially sighted people, special raised markings may be required.)

Check that the control is easy to operate. As with door handles, a small smooth round knob is the most difficult. A square or flanged control is easy to grip and manipulate, and deep grooving helps those with poor co-ordination. The type of control on a television set is important. For those with arthritic hands or poor co-ordination, any type of gradual adjustment is unsuitable. A clear-cut transition from one channel to another is easiest, preferably operated by simple pressure on the appropriate knob.

A pneumatically controlled or one-switch radio is now being developed for those who have difficulty in operating normal radio controls. The user can select six pre-tuned VHF stations (tunable to suit the locality) and adjust the volume level. To operate the radio, the user puffs or presses the microswitch the required number of times until he reaches the station. The radio will operate from the mains, or may be connected to a Possum control system, which is discussed below.

Communication

Communication falls into two distinct categories: the *call for help*, either as part of the daily routine (for assistance in the bathroom, for example), or in an emergency; and the natural *desire to communicate* with others.

The first need can be met fairly simply, assuming that there is someone else in the house, by means of a bell (hand or electric) or whistle, or by the installation of a baby alarm system, wired to whichever room or rooms are likely to be in use.

Both needs can, to a certain extent, be met by the installation of an intercom, which will not only summon help when required, but can also provide limited contact within the home.

A wider range of contact is afforded by the installation of a telephone, and this is especially important if the disabled person is likely to be alone for protracted periods, or if he has friends or working contacts outside the home. The Post Office makes various adaptations for those with hearing or seeing difficulties. There is also special equipment to help those who cannot dial calls for themselves or hold the receiver. This includes such aids as callmakers, which dial automatically from pre-programmed cards, to loudspeaking telephones, which can be adapted for use with a Possum control system.

A Possum unit is an extremely sophisticated system, supplied where appropriate by the National Health Service, which controls a variety of appliances and services: telephone, radio, television, typewriter, heating, lighting and door opening. It is operated by a simple suck/blow mechanism, or by light pressure on a switch. It is *not* available privately, and can be supplied on prescription only.

Communication is normally made by sound, but for some people this is completely useless. Those with hearing difficulties need other forms of signal, and this applies to door bells, telephone bells and the like. All these can have alternative light signals, and these will save a disabled person anxiety and embarrassment.

For those people for whom moving is slow and painful, an intercom system with a speaking tube and remote control to open the front door saves a great deal of effort.

Finally there is the debated question of personal alarm systems. Here there is no unanimity as to efficiency, and one of the main difficulties is that in many the equipment must be body worn. There are, however, various two-way systems which are worth consideration if someone else is normally in the house. A handicapped person living at home with other people must usually expect to depend on those people rather than on any mechanical contrivance.

A Possum control system can be used to operate a wide variety of appliances and services. Here a tetraplegic man is using the suck/blow mechanism to work an electric typewriter.

Chapter 9
Recreation

Recreation is one of the most important parts of a handicapped person's life and may range from gardening to listening to records, from dressmaking to writing. Whatever it may be, it should be encouraged and taken seriously, and a real attempt should be made to foster it. Part of the enjoyment of anything worth doing *is* the effort involved, but everyone needs a certain amount of success.

Most people who have recently become disabled will almost certainly have had some hobby or pursuit, and they must investigate the practicability of continuing this, though perhaps in a modified form. Gardening, for example, is possible in a variety of ways, ranging from outdoor work to indoor or greenhouse activities.

While disablement debars one from some hobbies, it may give increased time and opportunity for others. These include such pursuits as drawing, painting and writing, studying a new language, craft or academic subject, and possibly learning to play a musical

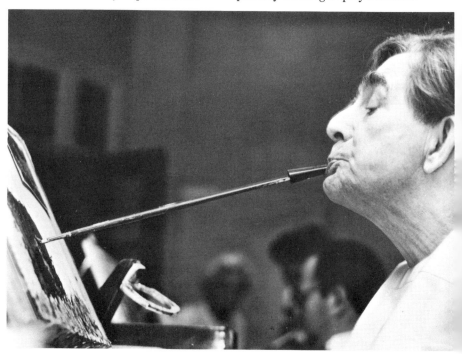

instrument. There are also vastly increased opportunities for listening to both the radio and recorded music.

If you decide to carry on an existing hobby, then it is worth while buying special equipment or adapting present conditions. If you choose a new hobby, however, it is wise to go slowly and not spend large sums of money on something that may be only a passing fancy. In any case, too elaborate provision of facilities may well daunt the prospective user. A drawing block and sticks of charcoal, or a set of colour pencils, will be more encouraging to the novice than an easel and a box of oil paints.

Provision for a hobby may consist merely of space for books or a cupboard for outdoor equipment (angling, for instance); or it may involve considerable changes, as for example in erecting a greenhouse or altering the layout of the garden. The greater the changes and the expenditure, the surer one needs to be of continuing interest.

Some hobbies will involve and benefit other members of the family, for instance the provision of hi-fi equipment; and this may best be sited in a shared room, such as the living room. Other pursuits may be more solitary, for example writing or painting, where equipment should preferably be kept in a bedroom or study. Where possible, however, it is well to involve other people, so that the handicapped person has the opportunity to share his interests and pass on his knowledge. A keen bird-watcher can lend his binoculars and

CAMILLA JESSEL

53

describe the different birds; a gardener can provide cuttings or seedlings, or give expert advice; someone who does embroidery or sews well can help out an inexperienced friend.

Gardening is one pursuit which can be followed in a variety of forms, both indoors and out. For a keen gardener who is newly disabled, various changes in the garden may be necessary, depending on the type of disablement. It will almost certainly be necessary to raise the level of the garden beds, and probably to change the nature and width of the paths. Disused sinks are admirable for alpine plants and for many types of annual – they can be raised to a convenient height with bricks. Beds can

sections. Strawberries, herbs and alpine plants can be grown in strawberry pots or barrels. Peat walls can be built up with peat-loving plants in the crevices. All of these need special treatment, and can provide great interest.

Raised flower beds at one of the John Grooms Housing Association estates.

The Rosum Easygrow system of raised flower beds was developed for wheelchair users and people who have difficulty in bending. The beds are free standing, and there is plenty of room underneath for the disabled person's knees. By Easygrow Systems

be built up using bricks or old railway sleepers to retain them. New beds can be formed with old tyres or drain pipe

So far as paths are concerned, these must be wide enough for both a wheelchair user and an ambulant person using a stick or crutches (99 to 114cm). They should have a non-slip surface with a roughened or corrugated finish although this does *not* apply to a wheelchair user who propels his chair manually, in which case the finish should be reasonably smooth); and a ramp if the disabled person is in a wheelchair or, if ambulant, prefers a ramped surface to steps with side rails. The gradient of the ramp should be about one in twelve, and both a kerb and side rail should be provided.

A greenhouse is often a great pleasure to a handicapped person, as it provides an opportunity for specialised gardening, and also an even temperature for working. Obviously, if the handicapped person is in a wheelchair, care must be taken to ensure that the greenhouse is accessible, and staging must be at the right height for working, with sufficient space underneath for the user's knees.

Indoors, various forms of gardening are possible, ranging from the 'window greenhouse' type to bottle gardens or window boxes which require little effort.

Advice on all aspects of gardening is available from the Disabled Living Foundation, together with lists of special tools (see also Appendix C).

So far as bird-watching is concerned, the main home provision is for a feeding table at a height which is both safe for the birds and visible from a suitable window. The table should be stable and of a reasonable size, preferably with a shallow ledge so that food is not pushed off by greedy feeders. If possible, there should be space for hanging nut-feeders, coconuts or lumps of fat, as these will attract different varieties of bird. Membership of the Royal Society for the Protection of Birds (see Appendix B) will add to the bird-watcher's interest and knowledge, and advice on suitable tables, nesting boxes and other aids is available.

Two garden tools which are most convenient for handicapped people. The one-handed shear (left) can be used from a wheelchair, and the stainless steel swoe (right) is long enough for people who have difficulty in bending. Both tools by Wilkinson Sword

Listening to recorded music is a restful and enjoyable pastime which can be shared by the whole family. As with any major equipment, you generally get what you pay for, but the speakers are a matter for individual choice because they vary so much in character. The quality of sound depends on where they are used, so it is better to try them out at home before buying. If they are directional speakers there will be one most favoured position, and this should be where the handicapped person will sit, either in his wheelchair or in an easy chair. Some turntables have an automatic cueing device for records, and this can be invaluable for people with poor co-ordination.

For some disabled people (spastics and those with poor co-ordination), cassettes will be easier to handle than records, and less liable to damage. Many lending libraries also have a music section and it is worth enquiring whether they lend cassettes as well as records. Storage for cassettes and records must be convenient and accessible, and various types should be investigated to see which is the most suitable.

More solitary hobbies include drawing and painting, sewing and embroidery, all of which can be followed in a 'shared' room or in a study. Writing, learning a language (either by direct tuition, with records or tapes, or by following a course on the radio or television) and other studies must all be pursued in private, preferably in a study with the necessary equipment and reference books. Little or no special provision is required here, although if one is serious about dressmaking, both equipment and space are important. The choice of a sewing machine is a matter for careful consideration and trial; many firms are extremely helpful about modifications. A long mirror, possibly a dress form, hem marker, large table for cutting out, iron and ironing board must all be provided. In addition, in common with other pursuits involving close work, a really good and efficient light source is necessary; indeed, there should ideally be a light over the sewing machine, a floor or table lamp to illuminate hand sewing, as well as good general lighting for cutting out, fitting and so on.

Both pottery and woodwork are activities which may have to be modified, but which can still give a great deal of pleasure and interest (and possibly financial reward also). Full details of planning hobby rooms are given in *Rooms for recreation,* another book in this series, and specific notes for the disabled are included.

One hobby which may present considerable difficulties, but is worth following up, is the keeping of a pet. Even a badly disabled person or a child with little independent movement will enjoy watching a tropical fish tank or a pair of budgerigars in a cage. Every effort should be made to give the disabled person responsibility for the welfare of the pets, either by feeding them or keeping the timetable for their care. Other fairly undemanding 'pets' or living interests are a formicarium (containing ants), a vermarium (for worms) or an aquarium with newts. Any of these could be set up in a comparatively limited space, so long as they are within sight of the disabled person's usual position in the room, whether he is in bed or in a chair.

Kittens and puppies are much more demanding pets, particularly if they are not yet house trained. If the major part of the responsibility is to be undertaken by the disabled person, then it is almost essential that the animal has access

57

There are many other hobbies and pursuits which have not been discussed, as they involve little or no design alteration. Any activity which involves the disabled person in something other than his own normal life, and which also brings him into contact with the outside world, should be encouraged.

(through a cat door) to an enclosed garden or courtyard, where it can come and go at will. In choosing a dog, its need for exercise should be considered. A poodle, for example, will happily trot along beside a wheelchair, but unless a large garden is available more active breeds would soon become frustrated and unhappy. Just as a guide dog is far more than an essential mobility aid to his blind master, so a pet can become a close friend to a handicapped person, particularly if he has to spend long periods alone.

59

Chapter 10
Independence

Throughout this book, the aim has been to encourage the disabled person to live as full and independent a life as possible. Obviously this will vary tremendously according to his physical ability, age and character. In general, however, it is true to say that many handicapped people are capable of, and benefit from, a considerable amount of individual effort, which normally they are not called on to undertake.

Just as it is quicker and easier to feed a child, or put on his shoes and socks (and often less messy!), so one does things for a person who is slow or unco-ordinated in his movements. However, it becomes fatally easy to *take over* from a disabled person, leaving him no responsibility for his own life. If one is disabled, there are obviously some tasks which one cannot undertake, but these can be assessed. Some, involving problems of reach, control or access can be resolved; others may prove insoluble. Nothing should be dismissed as impossible or too difficult until it has been carefully considered, and advice sought either from a body such as the Disabled Living Foundation, or from a professional person such as a GP, physio- or occupational therapist. Many disabled people can triumph over seemingly insuperable odds.

Living is difficult enough for the handicapped person without adding to his obstacles. There are many ways in which routine tasks can be eased or even, in some cases, avoided altogether. There will be some things which he may find impossible or unnecessarily exhausting, and these should be done by other means, as a form of planned dependence. All of us rely on other people to a greater or lesser extent, and the family unit emphasises this inter-dependence. Each member, while leading his own life, should play his part in family living and feel he has a worthwhile role in the structure.

Personal needs and hygiene: bathing, dressing and so on, are essential parts of independence, and should be made as easy as possible for the disabled person. He should have every opportunity for personal fulfilment, in his hobbies and interests, for mobility, and for communication. He should share the general pattern of living, and accept responsibility for his part of the whole scheme.

Because of his disability, it is likely that the handicapped member of the family will have to accept a good deal of help. It is important, therefore, that he should have opportunities to give. These should, where possible, cover one aspect which he can look on as his own: answering the telephone and taking messages, preparing vegetables or a meal for working members or making jam or cakes, watering and tending indoor plants, raising vegetable or flower seedlings, and innumerable other necessary but time-consuming jobs. Whatever the field, it should be the handicapped person's own province and he should be given both the credit and the full responsibility.

Health and welfare services

A patient's doctor should be the person first consulted on matters of health and should advise on the availability of help from the various health services, including district nurses, health visitors, physio- and occupational therapists and specialist clinics.

District nurses visit patients in their own homes, and help with general nursing problems, including advice on relevant aids.

Health visitors visit in an advisory capacity.

Physiotherapists give treatment, either in the home or in the hospital out-patient department, on the recommendation of the patient's doctor.

Occupational therapists on the local authority (or attached to the hospital where the disabled person is a patient) advise on appropriate aids and recommend any necessary structural alterations. A grant towards the cost of these may be available through the local social services department, who should be able to suggest where equipment or appliances can be tested before purchase.

Low vision clinics supply aids and advice, on referral from the ophthalmic department of the patient's hospital.

Social services

These include social workers, home helps, Meals on Wheels and, in some local authorities, laundry services, especially where the patient is incontinent.

Disabled Living Foundation

The Disabled Living Foundation has a comprehensive exhibition of aids, which can be visited by appointment. There is also an information service to which anyone can apply for help and information.

Appendix B
Useful organisations

Age Concern England
(National Old People's Welfare Council)
Bernard Sunley House
60 Pitcairn Road
Mitcham
Surrey
01-640 5431

Association for Spina Bifida and
Hydrocephalus
Devonshire Street House
30 Devonshire Street
London W1
01-486 6100

British Council for Rehabilitation of the
Disabled
*(now merged with Central Council for the
Disabled to form Royal Association for
Disability and Rehabilitation, see below)*

British Epilepsy Association
3 Alfred Place
London WC1
01-580 2704

British Polio Fellowship
Bell Close
West End Road
Ruislip
Middlesex
Ruislip 75515

British Red Cross Society
9 Grosvenor Crescent
London SW1
01-235 5454

British Rheumatism and Arthritis
Association
6 Grosvenor Crescent
London SW1
01-235 0902

Central Council for the Disabled
*(now merged with British Council for
Rehabilitation of the Disabled to form
Royal Association for Disability and
Rehabilitation, see below)*

Chest, Heart and Stroke Association
Tavistock House North
Tavistock Square
London WC1
01-387 3012

Design Council
28 Haymarket
London SW1
01-839 8000

Disabled Living Foundation
346 Kensington High Street
London W14
01-602 2491

Disablement Income Group
Attlee House
Toynbee Hall
28 Commercial Street
London E1
01-247 2128

Down's Children's Association (Mongol
children)
Quinborne Centre
Ridgacre Road
Quinton
Birmingham 32
021-427 1374

Greater London Association for the Disabled
1 Thorpe Close
London W10
01-960 5799

Ileostomy Association of Great Britain and
Ireland
Drove Cottage
Fuzzy Drove
Kempshott
Basingstoke
Hampshire
0256 21288

Invalid Children's Aid Association
126 Buckingham Palace Road
London SW1
01-730 9891

Lady Hoare Trust for Physically
Handicapped Children
7 North Street
Midhurst
Sussex
073081 3696

Multiple Sclerosis Society
4 Tachbrook Street
London SW1
01-834 8231

Muscular Dystrophy Group
35 Macaulay Road
London SW4
01-720 8055

National Association for Mental Health
22 Harley Street
London W1
01-637 0741

National Association for Deaf/Blind and
Rubella Handicapped
164 Cromwell Lane
Coventry 4
0203 462579

National Deaf Children's Society
31 Gloucester Place
London W1
01-486 3251

National Elfrida Rathbone Society (ESNM)
83 Moseley Street
Manchester 2
061-236 5358

National Fund for Research into Crippling
Diseases
Vincent House
1A Springfield Road
Horsham
Sussex
0403 64101

National Society for Autistic Children
1A Golders Green Road
London NW11
01-458 4375

National Society for Mentally Handicapped
Children
Pembridge Hall
17 Pembridge Square
London W2
01-229 8941

Parkinsons Disease Society of The United
Kingdom
81 Queens Road
London SW19
01-946 2500

Pre-School Playgroups Association
Alford House
Aveline Street
London SE11
01-582 8871

Joseph Rowntree Memorial Trust
Family Fund
PO Box 50
York
0904 29241

Royal Association for Disability and
Rehabilitation
23/25 Mortimer Street
London W1
01-637 5400

Royal National Institute for the Blind
224 Great Portland Street
London W1
01-388 1266

Royal National Institute for the Deaf
105 Gower Street
London WC1
01-387 8033

Royal Society for the Prevention of
Accidents
Cannon House
The Priory Queensway
Birmingham 4
021-233 2461

Royal Society for the Protection of Birds
The Lodge
Sandy
Bedfordshire
0767 80551

Scottish Council for the Care of Spastics
22 Corstorphine Road
Edinburgh 12
031-337 2616

Scottish Information Service for the
Disabled
18-19 Claremont Crescent
Edinburgh 7
031-556 3882

Spastics Society
12 Park Crescent
London W1
01-636 5020

Spinal Injuries Association
126 Albert Street
London NW1
01-267 6111

Thistle Foundation
22 Charlotte Square
Edinburgh 2
031-225 7282

Toy Libraries Association
Sunley House
10 Gunthorpe Street
London E1
01-247 1386

Women's Royal Voluntary Service
17 Old Park Lane
London W1
01-499 6040

Appendix C
Suppliers of aids and appliances

Aids for the deaf

A F Bulgin & Co Ltd
Bypass Road
Barking
Essex

Frank Estcourt
22 Connaught Avenue
Manchester 19

Highfields Centre
26 Allensbank Road
Heath
Cardiff

Hector Tanner & Co
153 West Street
Bristol 3

Wytec Ltd
20 Stapenhill Road
North Wembley
Middlesex

Bathing aids

Carters (J & A) Ltd
Westbury
Wiltshire

F Llewellyn & Co Ltd
Carlton Works
Carlton Street
Liverpool 3

Surgical Medical Laboratory
Manufacturing Ltd
Bath Place
High Street
Barnet
Hertfordshire

Baths

Medic-Bath Ltd
Ashfield Works
Hulme Hall Lane
Manchester 10

Nicholls & Clarke Ltd
Niclar House
3/10 Shoreditch High Street
London E1

Communications

Benross Trading Co Ltd
Benross House
74-82 Rose Lane
Liverpool 18

Coventry Controls Ltd
Godiva House
47/49 Allesley Old Road
Coventry 5

Davis Safety Controls Ltd
Brunswick Industrial Estate
Newcastle upon Tyne

Diktron Developments Ltd
5 Highgate Square
Birmingham 12

Entryphone Co Ltd
172 Ifield Road
London SW10

Hadley Sales Services
112 Gilbert Road
Smethwick
Warley
West Midlands

Pifco Ltd
Pifco House
Failsworth
Manchester 35

Post Office Telecommunications
(address of Telephone Sales Office is in
local telephone directory)

Ramat & Co
30 City Road
London EC1

Sentrymatic Ltd
Queens Grove
St Johns Wood
London NW8

Sterdy Telephones Ltd
Plumpton Road
Hoddesdon
Hertfordshire

West London Direct Supplies
PO Box 595
169 Kensington High Street
London W8

Wytec Ltd
(address above)

Door and drawer furniture

G & S Allgood Ltd
Carterville House
297 Euston Road
London NW1

Dryad Metal Works Ltd
40/42 Sanvey Gate
Leicester

Newman-Tonks Ltd
Hardware Division
Allesley Street
Aston
Birmingham 6

Nicholls & Clarke Ltd
(address above)

Josiah Parkes & Sons Ltd
Union Works
Gower Street
Willenhall
West Midlands

Electric controls and switches

Brailled controls and other adaptations are
available from local Electricity Board
showrooms

B B I Lighting Ltd
Rankine Road
Daneshill Estate
Basingstoke
Hampshire

Fotherby Willis Electronics Ltd
Gladstone Terrace
Stanningley
Leeds
Yorkshire

Herga Electric Ltd
Northern Way
Bury St Edmunds
Suffolk

M K Electric Ltd
Shrubbery Road
Edmonton
London N9

Newton Aids Ltd
2A Conway Street
London W1

Superswitch Electric Appliances Ltd
7 Station Estate
Blackwater
Near Camberley
Surrey

Walsall Conduits Ltd
Excelsior Works
Dial Lane
West Bromwich
West Midlands

Furniture

Bedroom
Kewlox Furniture Ltd
Top Crest House
Delamare Road
Cheshunt
Hertfordshire

F Llewellyn & Co Ltd
(address above)

Paramount Kitchen Furniture
(Northern) Ltd
Paramount House
Brampton
Carlisle
Cumbria

Surgical Medical Laboratory
Manufacturing Ltd
(address above)

Kitchen
George A Moore & Co Ltd
Thorpe Arch Trading Estate
Wetherby
West Yorkshire

Multyflex Kitchens Ltd
Design and Planning Centre
North Dock
Llanelli
Dyfed
Wales

Nicholls & Clarke Ltd
(address above)

Paramount Kitchen Furniture
(Northern) Ltd
(address above)

Garden equipment

Easygrow Systems
9 Hamilton Road
London W5

Stanley Garden Tools Ltd
Woodhouse Mill
Sheffield 13

Wilkinson Sword Ltd
Sword House
Totteridge Road
High Wycombe
Buckinghamshire

Gas controls

Brailled controls and other adaptations are
available from local Gas Board showrooms.
Local service centres can arrange for a home
service adviser to make a free home visit

Greenhouses

Alton Glasshouse Ltd
Alton Works
Bewdley
Worcestershire

Hoists

S Burvill & Son
Primrose Road
Hersham
Surrey

Mecanaids Ltd
St Catherine Street
Gloucester 1

F J Payne & Son Ltd
Mill Street
Osney
Oxford

Wessex Medical Equipment Co Ltd
108 The Hundred
Romsey
Hampshire

Left-handed equipment

Anything Left Handed Ltd
65 Beak Street
London W1

Lifts

Terry Personal Lifts
Knutsford
Cheshire

Wessex Medical Equipment Co Ltd
(address above)

Ramps

Expamet Industrial Products Ltd
16 Caxton Street
London SW1

Homecraft Supplies (Fleet Street) Ltd
27 Trinity Road
London SW17

Kimberley Bingham & Co Ltd
111 High Street
Bordesley
Birmingham 12

Nottingham Handcraft Co
17 Ludlow Hill Road
Melton Road
West Bridgford
Nottingham 2

Rootes Maidstone
Mill Street
Maidstone
Kent

Simcross Services
4 Hollywell Road
Watford
Hertfordshire

H C Slingsby Ltd
89/95/97 Kingsway
London WC2

South Western Industrial Research Ltd
(Swirl)
University of Bath
Claverton Down
Bath 2

Sanitary aids

Carters (J & A) Ltd
(address above)

Clos-O-Mat (GB) Ltd
2 Brooklands Road
Sale
Cheshire

F Llewellyn & Co Ltd
(address above)

Mecanaids Ltd
(address above)

Medic-Bath Ltd
(address above)

Nicholls & Clarke Ltd
(address above)

Surgical Medical Laboratory
Manufacturing Ltd
(address above)

Showers

Armitage Shanks Ltd
Armitage
Staffordshire

Chiltern Medical Development
(Equipment) Ltd
Southern Road
Thame
Oxfordshire

Nicholls & Clarke Ltd
(address above)

Transport

Braune of Stroud
Griffin Mill
Thrupp
Stroud
Gloucestershire

Appendix D
Wheelchair sizes and requirements

Building requirements

Ramps

Where possible, the approach from a path or garage to the house should be level for both the wheelchair user and ambulant person. In other cases the wheelchair user must be provided with a ramp; this may be suitable for the ambulant person also, but he may prefer shallow steps with hand rails on each side.

The gradient of any approach ramp to a house should not be steeper than 1 in 12 (approximately 5°). For gradients of between 1 in 12 and 1 in 15 (between 4° and 5°) the maximum length of the ramp should be 10m.

Where a ramp leading to an entrance door is steeper than 1 in 20 (approximately 3°), a level platform measuring at least 1m by 1.2m should be incorporated at the head. Unless this platform is under cover (which is preferable) it should be inclined to a slight gradient for surface water drainage (ie less than 1 in 20).

The ramp should be not less than 1m wide and a suitable upstand should be provided on any side where there is a drop. An ambulant user will need, and a wheelchair user will appreciate, a guard rail also. The ramp should *not* be made of wood; concrete with a slip-resistant surface such as a carborundum finish is suitable.

Garage

If possible there should be level, covered access from the garage to the house. The wheelchair user will need a clear space of not less than 2.8m for access and transfer.

Paths

Garden paths should be not less than 1m wide for the wheelchair user, and for the ambulant person they should be wide enough to provide a stable non-slip surface for crutches, walking frame or other appliance. For a disabled child using a wheeled device, the wheelchair width will be adequate. If necessary, a turning area should be provided.

The gradient of a path should be 1 in 20 (3°) if possible, and must not be steeper than 1 in 12 (approximately 5°). Provision as to upstands and rails should be as for ramps. The surface should be slip resistant, but should not be constructed of loose material such as gravel.

Doors and passages

The front door should give a clear opening of 750mm, although a wider one may be preferred. Raised thresholds should not be higher than 25mm, and consideration should be given to the incorporation of a recessed doormat. (This applies to both wheelchair and ambulant users.)

Internal doors should give 775mm clear openings. Passages should be not less than 900mm wide. In a room where a wheelchair is to be turned round, an unobstructed circular space of 1500mm is required.

Overall dimensions of wheelchairs

Self-propelled chairs	Width mm	Length mm
DHSS general purpose model 8GJ	585	1015
DHSS general purpose model 8BL	585	940
DHSS general purpose model 8L	630	1040
DHSS indoor chair model 1	635	940
E and J universal chair		
adult model	615	1040
junior model	565	1040
Attendant-propelled chairs		
DHSS car chair model 9	635	760
DHSS outdoor chair model 13	685	1295
E and J attendant-propelled chair	610	990
Electrically-powered indoor chairs		
DHSS EP1C	610	890
E and J Sleyride	570	940
BEC	635	735

Appendix E
Further reading

Aids for the handicapped
Nicholas D B Elwes
The Spastics Society, 1973

Aids to independence
Central Council for the Disabled

Clothes sense for handicapped adults of
all ages
P Macartney MAOT
Disabled Living Foundation, 1973

Clothing for the handicapped child
Gillian Forbes
Disabled Living Foundation, 1971

Coping with disablement
Peggy Jay MBAOT SROT
Consumers' Association, 1974

DESIGN magazine
Published monthly by the Design Council

Designing for the disabled
Selwyn Goldsmith
RIBA Publications, 3rd edition 1976

Directory for the disabled: a handbook
of information and opportunities for
the handicapped
Ann Darnbrough and Derek Kinrade
Woodhead-Faulkner, 1977

Dressing for disabled people
Rosemary Ruston
Disabled Living Foundation, 1977

Early years
Morigue Cornwell
Disabled Living Foundation, 1976

Easy cooking for one or two
Louise Davies
Penguin, 1972

Easy path to gardening
A S White et al
Reader's Digest, 1972

Electric aids for disabled people
Electricity Council booklet

Equipment for the Disabled booklets
Clothing and dressing for adults
Communication
Disabled child
Disabled mother
Hoists and walking aids
Home management
Housing and furniture
Leisure and gardening
Personal care
Wheelchairs and outdoor transport (special
supplement)

Everyday aids for the disabled
West Sussex Association for the Disabled

Footwear for problem feet
M D England OBE
Disabled Living Foundation, 1973

Footwear: what to get and where to get it
Marjorie Thornton
Disabled Living Foundation, 1976

Four architectural movement studies for the
wheelchair and ambulant disabled
Felix Walter
Disabled Living Foundation, 1971

A handbook for parents with a handicapped
child
Judith Stone and Felicity Taylor
Arrow Books, 1977

The handicapped person in the community
Ed D M Boswell and J M Wingrove
Open University, 1974

Help for handicapped people
Department of Health and Social
Security booklet

Home made aids for handicapped people
British Red Cross Society, revised 1974

How gas makes life easier for disabled
people
British Gas leaflet

Incontinence: a guide to the understanding
and management of a very common complaint
Dorothy Mandelstam
Heinemann Medical Books, 1977

An introduction to domestic design for the
disabled
Felix Walter
Disabled Living Foundation, 1969

Kitchen sense for disabled or elderly people
Sydney Foott, Marian Lane and Jill Mara
Heinemann Medical Books, revised 1977

Management of incontinence in the home:
a survey
Patricia Dobson SRN HV
Disabled Living Foundation, 1974

Outdoor pursuits for disabled people
Norman Croucher
Disabled Living Foundation, 1974

People in wheelchairs: hints for helpers
British Red Cross Society booklet

Play helps
Roma Lear
Heinemann Medical Books, 1977

Rooms for recreation
Euan Barty
Design Council, 1977

'So you are paralysed . . .'
Bernadette Fallon
Spinal Injuries Association, 1975

Spaces in the home: Bathrooms and WCs
Department of the Environment
Design Bulletin 24 Part 1
HMSO, 1972

Spaces in the home: Kitchens and
laundering spaces
Department of the Environment
Design Bulletin 24 Part 2
HMSO, 1972

Which? magazine
Published monthly by the Consumers'
Association